# It's All About The Light

## How to Find God in Tough Times

**Six life-changing choices**

By Joanna Watson

malcolm down

PUBLISHING

First published 2026 by Malcolm Down Publishing Ltd
www.malcolmdown.co.uk

29 28 27 26 7 6 5 4 3 2 1



British Library Cataloguing in Publication Data
A catalogue record for this book is available from the British Library.

ISBN 978-1-917455-57-2



Cover design by Esther Kotecha
Art direction by Sarah Grace
Back cover author photo by John Cairns Photography

Printed in the UK

This deeply moving yet practical book is a must-read for anyone going through tough times or walking alongside those who are. In such situations, Joanna reminds us, we can either let these things push us away from God, or draw us deeper into him. But to experience the latter, there are choices to be made; and through penetrating insights, moving stories and searching questions, all deeply rooted in Scripture, Joanna helps us unlock keys to navigating through such times and to finding God's *"light through the cracks"*. This outstanding book, which can be used either personally or in a group context, will certainly prove helpful to many and I warmly commend it.

**Revd Mike Beaumont**
**Bible teacher, author, broadcaster**

Navigating seasons of shadow and complexity, while retaining your ability to be positive but honest, is always challenging. But in this book Joanna inspires, instructs and helps us understand how to see light, even in the midst of darkness. Her six chapters are like bright stepping stones to guide us in those tough times. So, as you read and embrace her nuggets of wisdom and practical advice, allow your heart to seek; then find God to be faithful and kind, even in those tough seasons of life. This is a book that is easy to read and so relatable. Enjoy!

**Rachel Hickson**
**Director of Heartcry for Change**

This is an extremely helpful and practical book on a subject where we often find ourselves feeling helpless. How do we approach tough times, and how do we support friends and family in theirs? Joanna offers rich theological insights, laser-focused spiritual awareness, and plenty of tangible ways we can find God's light when life isn't easy. A highly useful guide for every Christian.

**Lucy Rycroft**
**Author and Founder of The Hope-Filled Family**

*It's All About the Light: How To Find God In Tough Times* is a meaty, truth-filled, deep-dive into Scripture on the subject of inviting God into our places of suffering. Illustrated with true-life stories and backed up with stories from the Gospels, it contains truths that can bring hope, build faith for the impossible, and provide a blueprint for victorious Kingdom living.

It is an immensely practical book, with places to pause and reflect, answer probing questions, and respond to the truth with action. A treasure trove of godly wisdom, suitable for both individual and group use.

Anyone who has lived through hard times, or who has watched a loved one suffer, will find help, comfort and guidance in the pages of this book, as Joanna points us to the One who is the Light in our darkness.

**Joy Margetts**
**Author, Bible teacher and Founder of Kingdom Story Writers**

This is such a helpful, wise and approachable resource. Joanna explores each theme like facets of a diamond, the light catching and revealing God's presence with us in life's toughest moments. Drawing from her own journey and weaving in authentic, inspiring stories from others, she reminds us that prayer is not formulaic but a relationship. So often it can feel as if we have no choice or agency when challenges come, but Joanna brings us hope and practical wisdom. She helps us to encounter God and discover ourselves within the narratives of Scripture.

One chapter that particularly resonated with me was "Lean In", which reflects on the strength of community and the transformative power of communal prayer. During one of the darkest seasons of my life, I was upheld by the prayers and care of faithful friends who carried me. Through this book, I am freshly inspired and given practices to help me as I uphold others with this kind of faith-filled prayer.

As you read, may you remain open to the gentle promptings of the Holy Spirit, who will draw your attention and speak to your heart. May his light sweep into any darkness and his loving presence shine through you and to those around you.

**Revd Sarah Whittleston**
**Elim National Prayer Director, Head of Prayer and Leadership Development at Elim Life Church in Kingstanding, Birmingham**

Joanna has delivered a highly readable and practical manual on how to walk with God through tough times. Her book is full of wisdom and biblical principles, and there is a welcome emphasis on listening to God. It will make for excellent discipleship and small-group material, and contains suggested exercises and further reading. This book will grow your faith and help guide you through troubled waters. Joanna is the real deal!

**Revd William Stuart-Lee**
**Rector of Church of the Holy Spirit in Leesburg, Virginia, USA**

# Dedication

For my beloved dad, whose faith in Jesus was unwavering, even at the end.

# Contents

# Foreword

The Bible never pretends that life is easy but it does promise that God is present. The psalmist writes, "Even the darkness will not be dark to you . . . for darkness is as light with you" (Psalm 139:12). That is the heart of the Christian journey: not the absence of darkness, but the presence of God's light within it.

Every follower of Jesus discovers in time that faith does not float us above the challenges of life. We still live in the same world as everyone else – a world of unexpected phone calls, unwelcome diagnoses, strained relationships and uncertain futures. Yet we walk through it with a different Companion. Yes, the path is narrow, but it is never empty; and although there may be potholes, we do not fall into them alone.

Tough times can break into our lives suddenly – a tragedy, a crisis, a moment that rearranges everything. They can also drift in slowly, almost imperceptibly: financial pressures that silently grow heavier, relational tensions that gradually fray our peace, health worries that creep into daily life. Whether sudden or slow, the question inevitably rises in the human heart: "If God loves me, why is this so hard?"

Part of the struggle is that many Christians feel unable to talk about tough times at all. We fear that acknowledging them makes us appear weak or faith-less. We avoid conversations that feel too heavy. And, in many churches, the topic rarely makes it into the sermon series. Yet Scripture speaks to it repeatedly. To prepare ourselves biblically for tough times isn't a sign of doubt, it is an act of wisdom. Just as a first-aid kit in the home doesn't mean we expect disaster, so thinking through suffering beforehand helps us respond with faith when – not if – hardship comes.

It is precisely for that reason that I welcome this immensely helpful and deeply practical book. I loved Joanna Watson's previous work, *Light Through the Cracks: How God Breaks In When Life Turns Tough*, with its honest and uplifting accounts of God's interventions. *It's All About the Light: How to Find God in Tough Times* goes further – it broadens the lens beyond "miracles" to explore the many ways God meets us, strengthens us, steadies us, and sometimes simply sits with us in the dark until the dawn breaks.

Let me highlight five qualities that struck me as I read.

### 1. This is a serious book

Tough times demand more than clichés. Joanna resists easy answers and acknowledges that some pits are climbed out of slowly, not instantly. She recognises that some sufferings remain unexplained and that God's ways can be mysterious. And she wisely reminds us that, in a culture of individualism, we sometimes need the strength and support of others.

### 2. This is a submissive book

We are not offered techniques to coerce God or formulas to guarantee outcomes. Instead, Joanna continually reaffirms that God remains sovereign, loving and wise. Faith does not manipulate God; faith trusts him.

### 3. This is a spiritual book

The light we seek is not found in ourselves but in God. Joanna emphasises the work of the Holy Spirit – comforting, guiding, illuminating – and invites us, when the dawn comes, to give God the glory and tell the story.

### 4. This is a scriptural book

Rooted deeply in God's word, Joanna draws on biblical narratives and principles – not as detached proof texts, but as living wisdom. The Bible is allowed to speak in its own voice, in its own context, and its authority shines through.

### 5. This is a sensitive book

Joanna understands that suffering is not one-size-fits-all. Some experience sudden, dazzling answers to prayer that even sceptics call miracles; others walk a slower path marked by perseverance and grace. She treats both journeys with compassion. She also acknowledges that tough times can bruise our faith, and she gently encourages readers to rediscover "the joy of their salvation".

The theme of light runs through both of Joanna's books, and how fitting that is. Whether read personally or used in a small group, this book has enormous potential to bring God's light into the shadows of life. May it comfort, strengthen and heal all who open its pages.

*Revd Canon J.John*
Evangelist, Author and Broadcaster

# Introduction

*"The light shines in the darkness,*
*and the darkness has not overcome it."*
(John 1:5)

Sickness. Accidents. Bereavement. Relationship breakdown. Redundancy. Financial strain.

None of us can opt-out of tough times. They are an inevitable part of life. But how we navigate them matters.

Will we make wise choices? Will we be intentional about asking God to come and be with us in the midst of our tough times? Will we actively invite him to break in? Will we purposely look for his light, piercing through the cracks and penetrating the darkness?

Aristotle Onassis once notably said, "It is during our darkest moments that we must focus to see the light."

As a Christian, I believe "the light" we must focus on is Jesus, God personified, because the light he radiates can never be extinguished. It's why the Bible says, about Jesus, that *"the light shines in the darkness, and the darkness has not overcome it."*

It's also why, when it comes to our darkest moments, it's all about the light.

When life turns tough, God longs to break in – and this book will help you find him.

## How did this book come to be?

When I wrote my first book, *Light Through the Cracks: How God Breaks In When Life Turns Tough*, a collection of ten true stories, I did so for three reasons: to generate faith for miracles, to celebrate what God has done, and to activate an invitation to write.

What I wasn't expecting was to hear from two groups of readers, with requests.

The first group would tell me about their own challenging situations and ask for my advice about how to find God in the midst of what they were facing – clearly longing for miracles. The second group would say how reading the book had got them thinking, so could I please create some content around the issues raised by the stories – to help facilitate individual reflection, small group discussion, or both.

As I prayed about how to respond to both these groups of people, I sensed God giving me six biblical "principles" for how to find him in tough times, each one based on the stories in *Light Through the Cracks* – and I began to write this book.

A short while later, I was invited to speak for a week at Lee Abbey Devon,[1] and I identified six gospel stories, each of which demonstrated one of the "principles" being outworked

1. www.leeabbeydevon.org.uk, accessed 28 October 2025.

in the context of Jesus' ministry. These formed the basis of my talks, which I framed as "choices".

I then decided to weave the two strands of material together – the draft book content plus my Lee Abbey talks – and the result is what you now have in your hands.

## Why has this book been written?

I would like to suggest three reasons why I have written *It's All About the Light*:

*1. To offer* ***a firm foundation*** *for finding God in tough times*

The Bible contains a wealth of guidance for finding God in tough times. In understanding and applying these ageless truths to the situations we are facing, we can stand firm on the solid ground they provide. I want *It's All About the Light* to be rooted in the Scriptures.

*2. To offer* ***practical advice*** *for finding God in tough times*

People often ask me for tangible ways to find God in tough times, so I have sought to incorporate real-life illustrations and practical advice into every chapter. I want *It's All About the Light* to be full of achievable suggestions.

*3. To offer* ***fresh faith*** *for finding God in tough times*

When life turns tough, our circumstances can sometimes feel so overwhelming that God seems distant or absent. It's then that we need fresh faith to seek God, and find him, in the midst of what we are facing. I want *It's All About the Light* to raise faith for God to break in.

## How has this book been designed?

For ease of use, each chapter has been designed with the same clear structure:

- **Introduction:** Presenting each principle, framed as a choice.
- **WHERE:** Outlining where the idea for each principle originated.
- **WHY:** Teaching to show the Bible-based rationale for each principle, interspersed with real-life illustrations.
- **WHAT:** Narrative unpacking of a story from the Gospels, to show how each principle was outworked in Jesus' ministry, framed as a choice.
- **HOW:** Practical advice and suggestions for application.
- **Digging Deeper:** Exercise ideas, worship songs and further reading.

## Who should read this book?

*It's All About the Light* is for people who are going through tough times; for those who are supporting them; and for those who want to prepare in advance so that, when tough times come, they are ready.

It is suitable for *individuals* who want to reflect on the principles raised; *twos and threes* who want to study the principles together; and *small groups* (such as home groups, youth groups or book clubs) who want to work through the principles together.

## How should this book be read?

*It's All About the Light* is intended for use in an informal setting, with no set timescales, so that the material can be adapted to suit the needs of those reading it. For example, each chapter could be covered in the course of a single week or spread over several weeks if that feels more appropriate.

The chapters will make most sense if read in chronological order, as some of the teaching builds on what has been covered in previous chapters.

Each chapter is divided into short sections that end with a "pause". Whenever you can, I would encourage you to engage with the questions in these "pauses", as they have been designed to help you reflect on, and digest, what you have just read.

As you consider your answers to the questions, please jot down your answers, using a notebook or journal and pen (or a digital device with a note-taking function, ideally disconnected from the Internet to avoid distractions). If you have a Bible to hand, you can also look up any passages that are new to you.

For those of you who would like to engage with the material through an exercise, sung worship or further reading, please use the "Digging Deeper" sections for suggestions.

If you are using the book with other people (either as part of a two or three, or in a small group) please note the following:

- It will work best if everyone in the group has read the relevant chapter (or sections of the chapter) in advance of the meeting, so that they can come ready for discussion, with the material fresh in their minds.

- The leader of the meeting will need to decide, in advance, which chapter (or sections of the chapter) he or she would like the group to cover in the time available.
- The leader of the meeting might also want to consider, in advance, some of the likely answers to the questions, so that he or she can anticipate any unhelpful tangents and keep the discussion on track.
- Any of the "pause" questions can be used to generate discussion. But there are also additional questions at the end of each chapter, specifically intended for twos or threes and small groups.

## A note about terminology

Where the text mentions *Light Through the Cracks*, with capital letters, this is a reference to my book of the same title. By contrast, where the text speaks of "*light through the cracks*", all in lowercase lettering with inverted commas on either side, this is a shorthand expression to describe God breaking into a tough time.

## One final thought . . .

In writing this book, I have had to "live" its message: I have had to learn how to find God in my own tough times.

The spiritual battle has been intense; the testing severe. The pain, at times, has felt unbearable; the heartache relentless.

But even in my darkest moments, I have found God breaking in, bringing his "*light through the cracks*".

My longing is that this will be your experience too.

In reading this book, I hope it will encourage you to make wise choices; inspire you to keep focusing on Jesus; equip you to find God in your own tough times. And when things seem bleak, my prayer is that you will discover "it's all about the light".

*Joanna Watson*

CHAPTER 1

# Listen

## When life turns tough, what is God saying?

*"This is my Son, whom I love; with him*
*I am well pleased. Listen to him!"*
(Matthew 17:5)

### Introduction

When life turns tough, we face a choice.

Will we accept the circumstances? If professionals are involved, will we agree with what they are saying? Or will we listen to what God has to say, especially if it's contradictory? Will we hold on to God's view of our situation?

Facts have to be faced, but God's truth has to be chosen. It's a choice that starts when we learn to listen to what God is saying in the midst of our tough time.

## WHERE: Where did the principle of learning to listen originate?

In each of the healing[2] stories in *Light Through the Cracks*, God speaks to the people in the midst of their tough times – and all of them listen to what he says. It's a common theme throughout the book.

He speaks in a variety of ways – and the people, as they learn to listen, hear God's voice speaking through specific Bible verses, prophetic words of warning or encouragement, dreams and visions, insightful words of knowledge, the powerful lyrics of worship songs, God's audible voice and his still small whisper.

No matter the method, what is important is that God has something to say about each tough time – and he wants it to be heard.

When the people involved choose to listen to what God is saying, there is a powerful pivotal point on which each story hinges – where the tough time is turned around.

In "X-rays Never Lie", Chapter 2 of *Light Through the Cracks*, we read Keith's story.

Shortly after a stroke has left him paralysed down his right-hand side, a well-meaning doctor tells him he will never write again. But God speaks – and Keith listens.

God speaks through multiple Christian friends who write to Keith with the same Bible verse in their cards,

2. *Light Through the Cracks* contains various kinds of miracle stories, but this point relates specifically to the healing miracle stories

letters and emails: "For I am the LORD your God who takes hold of your right hand and says to you, Do not fear; I will help you" (Isaiah 41:13).

As he keeps repeatedly reading this verse, Keith has a choice. Will he accept the doctor's diagnosis that he will never write again? Or will he listen to what God is saying, trusting that God will take hold of his right hand, remove all fear and help him?

***Pause:***

- Can you recall a tough time, from your own or another person's experience, where God spoke? How did you, or those involved, listen and respond?

## WHY: Why do we need to learn to listen to God?

I would like to suggest three reasons:

- **Firstly, we need to learn to listen – because God is one who speaks**

Every person's voice is unique; it's one of the reasons why voice activation is such a powerful security mechanism – and God's voice is no exception.

Our challenge is recognising what God's voice sounds like, and the different ways in which he speaks. The more we do this during everyday life, in relationship with him, the easier it will be to hear him when tough times come – because it will feel like second nature.

In John 10:3-4 Jesus likens our relationship with him to sheep with their shepherd. "The sheep listen to his voice," he says. "He calls his own sheep by name . . . and his sheep follow him because they know his voice." Then later, in verse 27, "My sheep listen to my voice; I know them, and they follow me."

God's heart is for us to be like these sheep, in relationship with our shepherd, Jesus, learning to listen to his voice, hearing him calling us by name, recognising it is him speaking, and following where he leads.

Just as Jesus heard his Father speaking through the Scriptures,[3] and through his voice and the Holy Spirit,[4] so it can be the same for us.

God primarily speaks through the Bible, which contains the language of his heart and reveals the unchanging nature of his character. So the best way to learn to listen, and hear him speaking, is to read, study and meditate on the Bible.

God also speaks through the Holy Spirit, for example, in dreams, visions and prophecies. But nothing he says will ever contradict, supersede or undermine what he has said in the Bible, so the Bible will always be our plumb line for testing what we are hearing.

3. See Matthew 4:1-13 for an example. Note that the written Scriptures available to Jesus were contained in the Torah – the first five books of the Old Testament.
4. Matthew 3:16-17

In "Release From a Prison of Darkness", Chapter 10 of *Light Through the Cracks*, we read the story of Anna, the talented teenage dancer who became unwell with ME.

As she undergoes different treatments, her symptoms stubbornly stay the same or worsen, and the months turn into years. She frequently feels forgotten.

Her parents, Chris and Gillian, wonder whether their prayers for her will ever be answered. Gillian, in particular, is terrified for Anna's future, aware of an old school friend who was diagnosed with ME in her early teens and, thirty years on, is still living with the condition.

When God eventually speaks to Anna, she has become so familiar with his voice that she recognises it immediately – and she listens.

God's word to Anna enables her and her parents to keep holding on in hope.

***Pause:***

- In what ways has God spoken to you? Can you give some examples?

- **Secondly, we need to learn to listen – because God instructs us to listen**

In Matthew 17:5 Jesus is up a mountain with three of his disciples, when a cloud covers them and God's voice speaks from the cloud.

"This is my Son," he says. "Listen to him!"

Not: "This is my Son. Talk to him."
Not: "This is my Son. Ask him for things."
Not: "This is my Son. Give him your long list of requests."

Just simply: "This is my Son. Listen to him!"

Put yourself into the shoes of those three disciples. When this happens, they have been hanging out with Jesus for a while. Every day they are listening to his words – and trying to put them into practice. Yet here is this voice, with this message, coming from a source they cannot see – telling them that Jesus is his Son and instructing them to listen to him.

How must they have felt?

I would like to suggest that God comes to us with the same instruction: "Jesus is my Son," he says. "Listen to him!"

There's an urgency, an imperative, a sense in which it's a master-key that will unlock so many doors in our relationship with God. Because, like the disciples, the more we hang out with Jesus, the more our relationship with him will deepen, the more his voice will become familiar, the more we will hear what he has to say, and the more we will want to follow his lead.

Listening is an instruction that needs to be heeded.

In "All It Takes Is One Split Second", Chapter 4 of *Light Through the Cracks*, we read the story of a married couple, Adrian and Ruth, and their horrendous car accident.

In the weeks that follow the accident, as Adrian fights for his life in intensive care, God gives us a Bible verse to hold onto, which we share with those who are praying for him and Ruth: "[He] will not die but live, and will proclaim what the LORD has done" (Psalm 118:17).

We heed what God has said by repeatedly declaring this prophetic promise into the spiritual realm. As we do so, we find our faith rising, and we lift our eyes off the situation and onto Jesus, which deepens our relationship with him.

***Pause:***

- When you pray, who is doing most of the listening and what, if anything, might need to change? What do you do with what you hear God saying to you?

- **Thirdly, we need to learn to listen – because God wants us to hear his perspective**

In our tough times, knowing what God has to say lifts our eyes to see the situation from his perspective. It enables us to *accept the facts* in light of his word, *choose the truth* of his word, and *stand firm* on his word – because, as he says in Isaiah 46:11, "What I have said, that I will bring about; what I have planned, that I will do."

God's perspective is often different from ours but, what he promises, he will deliver. "'For my thoughts are not your thoughts, neither are your ways my ways,' declares the LORD. 'As the heavens are higher than the earth, so are my ways higher than your ways and my thoughts than your thoughts . . . So is my word that goes out from my mouth: it will not return to me empty, but will accomplish what I desire and achieve the purpose for which I sent it'" (Isaiah 55:8-11).

By listening to God's word about our situation, we hear the truth about it, and find a way through it – because Jesus is "the way and the truth and the life."[5]

Listening to God also raises faith for the miraculous.

Romans 4:17-18 contains an example, where we read of "God who gives life to the dead and calls into being things that were not." Then, "Against all hope, Abraham in hope believed and so became the father of many nations, just as it had been said to him."

Abraham and his wife were old and barren. Theirs was an extraordinarily tough time, in a culture that placed high value on having children. The facts dictated that they would never be able to conceive, let alone have many descendants.

Yet God promised Abraham, in Genesis 17:4-5, that he would become "the father of many nations". He revealed his thoughts about the matter. He called forth his plans and purposes. He spoke a word that seeded faith for the seemingly impossible.

And Abraham chose to believe God's promise. He looked at the facts from God's perspective. He held onto God's word – and his and Sarah's tough time was transformed.

5. John 14:6

In "Holding Onto a Prophetic Promise", Chapter 9 of *Light Through the Cracks*, we read the story of Henrik and Inger.

Shortly before Henrik is diagnosed with blood cancer, his wife, Inger, is given a prophetic word of warning and encouragement by a stranger at the end of a church service. "Such a hard day is coming. So hard!" the stranger says. "But you must hold on, because a day of joy is coming."

God speaks through the stranger – and Inger listens.

A short while later, she and Henrik have to make a choice. Will they face the facts that come with a prognosis of blood cancer? Or will they choose the truth of Jesus' prophetic promise, trusting that joy will follow the hardship that lies ahead?

***Pause:***

- If you are facing a tough time at the moment, what is God saying about it, and how willing are you to accept his perspective?

## WHAT: What is the biblical basis for learning to listen?

In Luke 8:40-56 we find an example of learning to listen being outworked in the story of Jesus and Jairus.

In this story, life turns tough for Jairus and he has a choice to make. Will he face the facts and accept what the circumstances are dictating? Or will he listen to God's word on the matter, spoken through Jesus?

He makes the choice to listen – and we can learn from his example.

It's a story that gives us three *keys* that we can use to *unlock* this principle of learning to listen.

- **KEY 1: Ask for Jesus' *presence* in your tough time (Luke 8:40-42)**

  Now when Jesus returned, a crowd welcomed him, for they were all expecting him. Then a man named Jairus, a synagogue leader, came and fell at Jesus' feet, pleading with him to come to his house because his only daughter, a girl of about twelve, was dying.

This story starts with Jesus returning to Capernaum from the other side of the Sea of Galilee – where he has just healed and delivered a man from multiple demons. This has so frightened the people there that they have begged him to leave. But here, the crowd can't wait to welcome him.

So it's here, on the shore by the Sea of Galilee, that Jairus approaches Jesus and begs him to come to his house. He knows that Jesus' presence will heal his daughter.

Jairus is one of the leaders of the synagogue, so he is highly esteemed in the community, respected and revered. Given his status and authority, it is likely he has already summoned the best physicians in the area, none of whom have been able to help.

But what matters more is that Jairus is also a father and, at this moment in time, he is facing every parent's worst nightmare. His only daughter is dying; she is only twelve years old.

In first-century Jewish culture, the age of twelve was when a girl became a woman and legally accountable for her own actions. She would also have entered puberty around that age; her menstruation would have begun – and her parents would have started making arrangements for her marriage.

All this means Jairus' daughter is on the threshold of being able to birth new life – but her own life is on the threshold of ending. It's the toughest of tough times, for what can be worse than the death of a child? There's nothing that seems more unnatural. Parents aren't supposed to bury their children; it's meant to be the other way around. When a child dies, it's like a full stop before the end of a sentence.

Jairus doesn't care about his status in the community. He doesn't care how undignified it is to throw himself onto the floor before Jesus. He doesn't care that, in a culture where elders are honoured, Jesus is younger than him. All he cares about is his dying daughter.

In desperation, he throws aside decorum, falls on his knees before Jesus and pleads with him, his heart breaking: "Please come! You're the only one who can help us. We need you. My daughter needs you. She needs your presence – before it's too late. Please!"

Jairus, this leader, is conceding his need of Jesus. He is recognising that Jesus carries the power of God. He is acknowledging that only Jesus' presence can transform his tough time.

But what adds to the drama is that Jairus' job, as a synagogue leader, would have included warning people about false teachers. He would have been fully aware of what the Jewish leadership thought of Jesus at that time, and how they considered his claims to be heretical. He may well have been joining them in telling people to avoid him.

Yet, here he is, flinging himself at Jesus' feet, throwing caution to the wind, damaging his public reputation, risking his position of leadership at the synagogue, ignoring his peers' claims that Jesus is a false teacher, and begging him to come to his home.

For those watching, it is shocking. They have never seen anything like it.

But Jesus agrees. He goes "on his way" with Jairus, the two of them walking together – followed by a throng of people who fall in step behind them.

Jairus is expectant. He is in Jesus' presence – and soon his dying daughter will be too – while the crowd just wants to witness what happens next.

***Pause:***

Maybe, like Jairus, someone you love is unwell and dying, or facing another type of tough time.

If this is you, Jesus understands what you are facing – and he longs to be invited in, to come and be present.

He knows that, with his presence in your tough time, you can learn to listen.

Will you do what Jairus did? Will you let go of your dignity, humble yourself and fall on your knees before Jesus, and acknowledge your need of him? Will you ask him for his presence to come and be with you?

If we want to learn to listen during our tough times, the first thing we need to do is ask for Jesus' presence.

- **KEY 2: Allow for Jesus' programme[6] in your tough time (Luke 8:42-48)**

  As Jesus was on his way, the crowds almost crushed him. And a woman was there who had been subject to bleeding for twelve years, and she had spent all she had on doctors, but no one could heal her. She came up behind him and touched the edge of his cloak, and immediately her bleeding stopped.

6. "Programme" in this sense is meaning "schedule" or "timetable".

> "Who touched me?" Jesus asked.
>
> When they all denied it, Peter said, "Master, the people are crowding and pressing against you."
>
> But Jesus said, "Someone touched me; I know that power has gone out from me."
>
> Then the woman, seeing that she could not go unnoticed, came trembling and fell at his feet. In the presence of all the people, she told why she had touched him and how she had been instantly healed. Then he said to her, "Daughter, your faith has healed you. Go in peace."

Can you imagine Jairus' frustration as this scene unfolds?

He wants Jesus to reach his home as quickly as possible – and every second counts. His dying daughter needs to be in Jesus' presence if she's going to have any chance of survival.

But now there's an interruption and delay.

Jairus is probably wondering whether Jesus understands the urgency. "Why are you stopping?" he might be thinking. "Why does it matter who touched you? Please hurry up!"

But God is showing Jairus that he needs to allow for Jesus' programme, not his own. He is showing him that Jesus always stops for the one; that delays are an inevitable part of journeying with Jesus; that interruptions need to be embraced.

And the reason for this particular interruption is perfectly valid. For in the midst of this densely packed crowd, a woman has touched Jesus and power has left him. A woman who has been haemorrhaging blood for the past twelve years. A woman who has spent all her money on doctors – which Luke, as a doctor, is keen for us to clock.

Loss of blood causes light-headedness, shortness of breath, weakness and fatigue. Her suffering would have been immense. Worse, if this was a gynaecological condition, she would have been deemed ritually unclean, unable to participate in society or worship at the synagogue. The shame and stigma would have been huge.

So, for her to be in this crowd is lonely – and risky. She is rendering everyone around her ceremonially unclean. If she is discovered, they will all have to wash their clothes, bathe, and avoid coming into contact with anyone else until evening. They will be furious and she will be ostracised. She is terrified.

But there is also significance in the intersection of these two stories and their twelve-year spans.

This woman started bleeding in the same year that Jairus' daughter was born. She has known nothing but sadness – while Jairus and his wife have known only happiness. She has been shunned from the synagogue – while he is one of the synagogue's leaders. Her reputation has been ruined through no fault of her own – while his reputation is impeccable.

Yet here they are, united in desperation, with Jesus their only option.

This woman has heard about Jesus. She knows he has power to heal. So, she works her way through the crowd, reaches out and touches the edge of his cloak.

At that time, every God-fearing Jewish man would have worn a rectangular cloth, a loose-fitting vest fringed with tassels, each representing his faithfulness and commitment to keeping God's Law.[7] It is likely one of these tassels, dangling down behind Jesus' back, that this woman clutches.

In doing so, she is violating God's Law about uncleanness. Yet she is also throwing herself on his mercy. It is an act of utter desperation – and instantly, her bleeding stops. She is healed.

She could have gone on her way without anyone knowing. But Jesus knows the difference between accidental touch and intentional touch. As God Incarnate[8], he knows that power has left him.

So, he pauses his journey to Jairus' house; he allows for the interruption; he adjusts the programme – even though Jairus must have been stressing about the delay.

As he looks around to see who has touched him, the woman comes forward, fearful and trembling. Maybe because she fears being rebuked for being ritually unclean. Maybe because she can't quite believe she has been healed. Maybe because she knows she can't just slip away – and she is petrified.

Yet Jesus is so kind and tender. He has time for her. He doesn't mind being stopped. "Daughter," he says, "your faith has healed you. Go in peace."

This woman, who has suffered constantly for twelve years – bleeding, broken, weak, ashamed and desperate – is,

7. "God's Law" refers to the Torah – the first five books of the Old Testament.
8. God embodied in human form

here, being publicly and compassionately affirmed by God Incarnate. He affirms her as "daughter", showing that he sees her as part of the "family" of God's people, no longer excluded from it because of her ritual uncleanness. He affirms her faith with a word that describes both "healing" and "salvation", showing that she has been both healed and saved – physically, relationally, emotionally and spiritually.

Why? Because now the bleeding has stopped, she is clean. She can worship at the synagogue again. She can mix in society again. And he grants her "peace", from the word "*shalom*", which speaks of "wholeness". It means she is "complete".

Yet, there is also a completeness about the way this happens in front of Jairus.

"Woman, I'd like to introduce you to Jairus, the ruler of the local synagogue. Since you've not been able to come for the last twelve years, you might not know each other.

"Oh, and Jairus, while we're here, would you be able to save this woman a seat? I think you'll be seeing her on a regular basis now, so how about helping to ease her nerves."

I think Jesus wants Jairus to see the purpose in this interruption, and not to be stressed by it. He is fully aware of the perceived delay, but no amount of "hurry ups" will hurry him up. He is never early, never late, only ever on time. We have to allow for his programme.

***Pause:***

Maybe, like Jairus, you're pleading with Jesus to hurry up and come into your situation – before it's too late. Maybe it feels as though the answers to your prayers are being delayed or interrupted.

If this is you, God is aware of your need. He knows the urgency. He knows you are waiting. He has heard your prayers and is on the way. But you need to allow for his programme. He is never early, never late, only ever on time.

Spend a moment now, handing Jesus your frustrations.

Alternatively, maybe, like the woman in this story, you have been waiting for years, or even decades, for your miracle. Maybe you feel forgotten, hidden or overlooked.

If this is you, God does not mind his programme being interrupted. He is happy to respond to your faith, no matter how small.

Spend a moment now, reaching out to Jesus.

If we want to learn to listen during our tough times, the first two things we need to do are ask for Jesus' presence and allow for Jesus' programme.

- **KEY 3: Accept Jesus'** ***promise*** **regarding your tough time (Luke 8:49-56)**

  While Jesus was still speaking, someone came from the house of Jairus, the synagogue leader. "Your

> daughter is dead," he said. "Don't bother the teacher anymore."
>
> Hearing this, Jesus said to Jairus, "Don't be afraid; just believe, and she will be healed."
>
> When he arrived at the house of Jairus, he did not let anyone go in with him except Peter, John and James, and the child's father and mother. Meanwhile, all the people were wailing and mourning for her. "Stop wailing," Jesus said. "She is not dead, but asleep."
>
> They laughed at him, knowing that she was dead. But he took her by the hand and said, "My child, get up!" Her spirit returned, and at once she stood up. Then Jesus told them to give her something to eat. Her parents were astonished, but he ordered them not to tell anyone what had happened."

How must Jairus have felt, seeing the member of his household approaching? The man's facial expression would have conveyed the bad news. "Your daughter is dead," he says.

This is probably the bleakest moment that Jairus will ever know. His daughter has succumbed to her sickness; all hope has gone. What parent, at this point, would not collapse to the ground and wail with grief?

"Don't bother the teacher anymore," the man says, the implication clear – Jesus is too late.

Jairus' desperation must have turned to anger, confusion and heartache. "Why, Jesus? Why did you have to stop?" And to the messenger: "Why did you have to tell me such terrible news in front of so many people? Why not wait until I got home?"

Yet it's in this moment, in the middle of his tough time, that Jairus learns to listen. "Don't be afraid," Jesus says to him, "just believe, and she will be healed." And Jairus has to choose to accept this promise.

It's like he's saying, "Listen to me, Jairus. Hear this as my word for what you are facing. I'm promising you now, I will heal her. Please try to trust me. Please try to accept what I'm telling you. Please try to believe that I'm telling you the truth."

If you were Jairus, how would you have responded?

Jesus' words must have sounded ludicrous: "What do you mean: 'Don't be afraid'? 'Just believe'? 'Please try to trust you'? How am I meant to do that? My precious daughter is dead. Don't you understand how I'm feeling?"

But Jairus needs to tune out his internal monologue and learn to listen. He is welcome to accept the facts, but he also needs to trust the truth of Jesus' promise – because Jesus' promises are always life-giving, trustworthy, true and tenderly delivered.

When they arrive at Jairus' home, we know from the parallel accounts given by Matthew and Mark that a large crowd has gathered there, loudly weeping, wailing and mourning.[9] Someone is playing a reed flute. The din is deafening.

9. This is still a common way of expressing grief in many parts of the world today, including in the Middle East and Sub-Saharan Africa.

Over this enormous volume of noise, Jesus speaks with power and authority: "Stop wailing," he says. "She is not dead but asleep." Perhaps he has to raise his voice a little, to be heard above the hubbub. It matters not who hears it. The promise is not for the onlookers; it's solely for Jairus.

But immediately, he is mocked. "What do you mean, asleep? Don't be ridiculous! She's dead!" We can hear the crowd laughing and jeering at Jesus, even as he says it.

But Jesus has spoken a better word – and his is the word that counts.

This is why, when life turns tough, the first thing we need to do is learn to listen to God. We need to know his take on the situation. No matter what the facts dictate, God is in control, and it's the truth of God's word that counts. It's this that Jesus wants Jairus to grasp – and he is giving him a choice. *Will he accept the facts? Or will he choose the truth?*

But the people don't understand this; they just laugh.

We have to assume that Jesus ignores them, because we know from the accounts in Matthew and Mark that he goes into the house, accompanied only by Jairus, his wife and three of the disciples, Peter, James and John.

Inside, he walks over to the twelve-year-old body lying motionless in bed. He disregards Jewish tradition, which would have deemed anyone touching a corpse to be unclean for seven days, and he takes her by the hand. Instead of her making him unclean, he makes her clean.

Then he speaks a command: "My child," he says, "get up!" The word he uses means "Arise!" Immediately, her spirit returns to her body. She wakes, stands, and eats some food.

God's truth has been pronounced, the spiritual atmosphere has shifted, the facts have been refuted, the girl's spirit has yielded to the power and authority of Jesus' words, and his promise to Jairus has been fulfilled.

Can you imagine it?

The text tells us that Jairus and his wife are astonished. Had they really believed Jesus' promise? Had they really trusted him to deliver? Had they really chosen to embrace the truth and reject the facts? I mean, who on earth raises someone from the dead simply by commanding them to come back to life?

Everything within them must have wanted to broadcast the news; to tell all their family, friends and neighbours about this incredible miracle. "Our daughter was dead, but now she's alive!"

Instead, Jesus urges them not to tell anyone about what has happened.

It may be that he didn't want this family's holy moment to become a public spectacle. It may be that he didn't want people to come chasing after him, in anticipation of witnessing other signs and wonders. We don't really know.

But what we do know is that Jairus has learnt to listen to Jesus in the midst of this tough time – by choosing to accept his promise.

***Pause:***

Maybe, like Jairus, you are in a situation where the facts and the truth are contradicting each other. "Your daughter is dead" is a fact. "She is not dead, but asleep" is the truth.

Facts state the obvious; truth states God's prophetic promise. Facts declare what man sees in the situation; truth declares what God sees. Facts are easy to grasp; truth takes time and discernment to grasp.

In your tough time, what are the facts, and what is God's prophetic promise of truth?

If you don't yet have a promise from God for your tough time, perhaps you could lean in and ask others to listen to God on your behalf.[10] Alternatively, you could take hold of a promise from the Scriptures that speaks directly into your situation, using a Bible concordance if helpful, and asking the Holy Spirit to lead your search.

Once you have a promise from God for your tough time, you just need to take hold of it, pronounce it – and keep on pronouncing it. Don't hold back! Declaring God's word has power and authority.[11]

Will you, like Jairus, accept Jesus' promise? Will you face the facts, but choose the truth?

10. See Chapter 2, "Lean In", for how to do this.
11. This is unpacked more in Chapter 6, "Testify".

If we want to learn to listen during our tough times, the three things we need to do are: ask for Jesus' presence, allow for Jesus' programme and accept Jesus' promise.

When Jairus started out that day he knew that Jesus could do the impossible, but he needed to experience it for himself. The pivot point came when Jesus made a powerful prophetic pronouncement over his daughter – and Jairus made a life-changing choice to face the facts but choose the truth.

## HOW: How can we learn to listen in practice?

The good news is that listening to God is a skill that can be learnt!

Listening is not the same as hearing, which is an inherent inborn ability. Hearing alone is not enough for authentic communication; listening is what makes it genuine. Hearing comes only through the ears; listening comes through the mind, via all the senses.

Similarly, listening to God comes when the Holy Spirit speaks to our spirit.

In Psalm 85:8 the psalmist confidently declares, "I will listen to what God the Lord says," before adding, "he promises peace to his people."

Would it not be amazing if we could all have the same self-assurance as this psalmist, knowing that, in listening to what God is saying, we will receive his promise of peace? Yet for many of us, learning to listen is difficult. In our 21st-century

Western culture, our lives are so busy that we struggle to pause long enough to listen to anyone, not even our closest loved ones – let alone God!

So, what can we do, practically, to learn to listen to God?

- **Learn to listen – by regularly reading the Bible**

The Bible is the plumb line for all that God says, and he will never contradict what has been revealed in the Scriptures. The more we read the Bible, the more we will get to know his character, and the more familiar we will become with his ways, his words and his works.

The more we study, memorise and meditate on the Scriptures, the more we will be able to recognise God's voice, the more we will be able to discern whether what we are hearing is in alignment with the Scriptures, and the more we will be able to listen with accuracy.

- **Learn to listen – by getting to know God's ways of speaking**

In the stories in *Light Through the Cracks*, God speaks in a variety of ways, including through specific Bible verses, prophetic words of warning and encouragement, dreams and visions, insightful words of knowledge, the powerful lyrics of worship songs, his audible voice and his still small whisper.

In addition, God can also speak through things like the beauty of creation, seeming "coincidences",[12] angelic visitations,

12. I like to call these "God-incidences" and Chapter 1 of *Light Through the Cracks* includes lots of examples.

miraculous signs and wonders, teaching and preaching, pictures and images. (But this is not an exhaustive list!)

The more familiar we become with the different ways God speaks, the more we will learn to listen to him communicating with us, and the more clearly we will hear his voice.

- **Learn to listen – by dealing with distractions**

In tuning into God's voice, we need to filter out any *inner* distractions – including silencing our thoughts, ignoring the opinions of others, and suppressing the voice of the Enemy who so often seeks to bring confusion, deception, doubt and harm.

We also need to deal with all *outer* distractions – by setting aside time, in a conducive environment, turning off our digital devices, removing ourselves from those who demand our time and attention, and keeping a notepad handy to jot down things that come to mind.

- **Learn to listen – by having an expectant attitude**

When we open our spirits to the Holy Spirit, submit to the lordship of Jesus and give God our full attention, we are making ourselves receptive to the possibility of him speaking to us. We are more likely to listen if we are attentive, committed and expectant, even when we don't feel like it. It will also help us discern, understand and interpret what we are hearing.

***Pause:***

- Which of the ways God speaks most resonates with you, and why?
- How willing are you to commit to practising listening to God? What things might you need to change to make this possible?

## Digging Deeper

Now could be a good time to practise learning to listen to God.

**Exercise**[13]

- Invite the Holy Spirit to speak.
- Choose a Bible passage of no more than ten verses. If you are unsure which one to use, ask God to guide you.[14]
- Read the passage, slowly and out loud. As you do so, wait on the Holy Spirit and listen, paying attention to anything that stands out.
- Pause and reflect on what you have noticed. Is there a word or phrase? Is there a picture emerging, in the mind's eye, related to it? What is God wanting to say?
- Ask God to keep speaking, and then re-read the passage, paying attention, pausing and reflecting. Repeat this process another two or three times.

13. This exercise is known as *"Lectio Divina"*.
14. A good place to start might be in the Psalms or the Gospels.

- Each time, note down what you sense God saying.
- Take time to read and pray about the things you have noted.

If you are doing this exercise with others, you could share the reading of the passage between you. You could also share what each of you senses God saying, and pray over it together.

## Worship Songs

- "Believe For It" by CeCe Winans, Dwan Hill, Kyle Lee and Mitch Wong.
- "Got To Tell Somebody" by Don Francisco.[15]

## Further Reading

- *Listening to God* by Joyce Huggett.
- *How to Hear the Voice of God* by Pete Greig.

### Additional questions for small groups

- How do we currently listen to God for each other? In what ways is it working, and in what ways could we do it better?
- If one of us is going through a tough time and struggling to hear God's voice in it, how can we step in and listen on their behalf?

15. This song is a dramatic retelling of Jairus' story from his perspective.

CHAPTER 2

# Lean In

## When life turns tough, who has God placed around you?

*"Join me in my struggle by praying to God for me."*
(Romans 15:30)

### Introduction

When life turns tough, we face a choice.

Who will we lean in on – ourselves, other people or God?

Will we go it alone, hunkering down, trusting in our own strength and self-sufficiency to see us through? Or will we ask God to carry us through, reaching out to our Christian brothers and sisters, requesting their support and inviting them to intercede alongside us?

The persevering prayer support of other believers is one of the things that will sustain us through a tough time, but we have to choose it. It's a choice that starts when we learn to lean in on the Christian community that God has placed around us.

## WHERE: Where did the principle of learning to lean in originate?

In each of the stories in *Light Through the Cracks*, God places a group of Christians around the people who are in the midst of a tough time – and all of them pray, collectively interceding with God for the situation to be transformed. It is a common theme throughout the book.

Each situation is different; each set of people is diverse. Prayer requests are communicated through a variety of methods – including text messages, email prayer chains, blog posts, church notices and word-of-mouth – and the responses are wide-ranging. They include prayer at home alone; prayer over the phone; prayer in twos and threes, or other small group gatherings; and even an entire church congregation standing together, corporately interceding as an integral part of Sunday morning services during the height of a life-and-death crisis of one of their members.

What unites this aspect of the stories is that God has placed Christian believers around those who are at the centre of each tough time – and he wants them leaning in on each other and interceding together for transformation.

When the people involved choose to lean in on their Christian community, whatever that looks like, and when they collectively start to persevere in prayer, it creates a powerful shift in each story – where faith is raised and the tough time starts to turn around.

In "Nothing Can Separate Us", Chapter 8 of *Light Through the Cracks*, we read Jed's story, in which he has a tragic hammock accident.

As soon as he is discovered, unconscious, his mum Lisa starts praying for his healing and recovery – while simultaneously mobilising prayer support from friends, relatives and members of their church family.

She communicates regularly using a mobile phone messaging app, and her texts are passed on to others. As Jed's story unfolds in real time, the network of intercessors keeps growing, with prayers offered up on his behalf from places all over the world.

Lisa knows that Jed needs Jesus to intervene and save his life – so she chooses to lean in on the Christian community that God has given their family.

***Pause:***

How can we recognise the Christian community that God has given us? How can we get them involved in praying for us in a time of crisis?

## WHY: Why do we need to learn to lean in?

I would like to suggest there are two reasons why we need to learn to lean in.

- **Firstly, we need to learn to lean in – because God has designed us to live life in community with others**

Back at the beginning, when God was creating the world, he declared, "It is not good for man to be alone. I will make a helper . . . for him" (Genesis 2:18). His plan from the outset was for us to do life together. He designed us as relational beings.

Nothing illustrates this more clearly than the way we read the word *you* in the Bible. How often do we assume that *you* in the text is *singular*, when it's actually *plural?*[16] It so often gets lost in our English language translations.[17] Imagine the journey of discovery we would go on in our reading of the Bible, if we were to recognise the times when the *you* in the text is God speaking and relating, not to an individual person, but to a group of people living in community!

If we are followers of Jesus, we are part of the body of Christ (1 Corinthians 12:25-27) and God expects us to be in unity with that body (Ephesians 4:2-6). He wants us to discover and deliver our role within the body; to use the gifts God

16. Some Bible translations now seek to distinguish between singular "you" and plural "you" by using "you yourselves" for the plural.
17. Jeremiah 29:11 is a good example: "'For I know the plans I have for you,' declares the LORD, 'plans to prosper you and not to harm you, plans to give you hope and a future.'" The "you" in this verse is plural. It is God speaking to the entire nation of Israel. It is intended for the collective people of God. Yet how many of us read the "you" here as singular, and apply it to ourselves as individuals?

has given us; to love and serve other members of the body (1 Peter 4:8-11).

We are also called to show concern and compassion for the other members of the body. When one part is suffering, the whole body suffers with it – in the same way as we feel the pain of a stubbed toe or broken arm.

No single body part can exist without all the other parts; it's a biological impossibility. And no individual Christian can survive without being in community with other believers; it's a spiritual impossibility. Our faith is meant to be nurtured in community with other Christians, each person contributing their unique gifts so that everyone else benefits – and there is nothing like a tough time for us to see this in action.

Leaning in matters – because God has designed us to live life together in community with others.

In "Hard Pressed But Not Crushed", Chapter 5 of *Light Through the Cracks*, we read the story of Jackie and her twin babies, who are born extremely prematurely.

As the trauma of the story unfolds, there are several moments when Jackie feels emotionally numb, unable to process what's happening. But she knows that her church community will pray for the twins, as will her other close Christian friends, of which I'm one. All she has to do is reach out and ask.

As Jackie learns to lean in on us in her time of need, we do what we can to support and carry her, and the twins, through our prayers and practical support.

***Pause:***

- Which Christian friends could lean in on you, and which ones could you lean in on, during a tough time?
- Have you ever considered how unique you and the gifts you carry are to the body of Christ? If you can't yet see what your "uniqueness" is, ask God to reveal it to you.

- **Secondly, we need to learn to lean in – because God wants us to intercede for each other**

Intercession is heartfelt prayer on behalf of others. It involves stepping into the gap for another person, or group of people, bringing their needs before God, crying out to him to intervene. It creates a bridge of connection between those who are in the midst of tough times and God, the only one who can turn their situations around.

It's an outworking of Galatians 6:2, which instructs us to "carry each other's burdens", and James 5:16, which urges us to "pray for each other so that you may be healed." It's a way of supporting and uplifting our friends, family, community, and even those we may not know personally.

In Exodus 17:8-15 we read a story where we see this in action. Set high on a hill, Aaron and Hur are holding up Moses' hands while, down in the valley below, Joshua and the Israelites are fighting a challenging battle against an enemy army. "As long as Moses held up his hands, the Israelites were winning," we read in verse 11, "but whenever he lowered his hands, the Amalekites were winning."

In his hands, Moses is holding high his staff, and this is significant. The staff represents God's power, through which miracles have been wrought in the history of God's people up to this point. It was when Moses raised his staff over the water that the Israelites escaped their Egyptian captors and crossed the Red Sea on dry ground; it was when he raised his arm and struck his staff against the rock in the desert that water gushed forth. So, Aaron and Hur know that Moses needs to hold high the staff over the battleground below if victory is to be won.

In modern-day parlance, it is equivalent to Aaron and Hur interceding, alongside Moses, supporting him to access God's power. Together, they are believing for a miracle on behalf of their community of believers who are battling through a tough time.

"When Moses' hands grew tired, they took a stone and put it under him and he sat on it," we read in verse 12. "Aaron and Hur held his hands up – one on one side, one on the other – so that his hands remained steady till sunset."

Put yourself into the shoes of Aaron and Hur, and notice the importance of their role. How must they have felt, supporting Moses at such a critical time?

How many of us are facing battles, not of the military kind but relational, emotional or spiritual ones, where we need God to come in power to turn them around? How many of us need an Aaron and a Hur to stand alongside us, interceding for us, believing with us for a miracle in the midst of our tough time?

Leaning in matters – because God wants us to intercede for each other.

In "Beautiful Inside and Out", Chapter 3 of *Light Through the Cracks*, we read the story of Rebecca and her complicated birth.

Her parents, Luca and Marianne, are praying, committing their unborn baby to God.

As soon as her due date approaches and, even more so after her birth becomes complicated, they also mobilise their Christian family and friends to pray – of which I am one. "Please pray," Luca's text reads at the start of the story. "The doctors don't think she's going to make it through the night. She probably hasn't got much longer left."

As we intercede for Rebecca, Luca and Marianne lean in on us, and we support and carry them through our prayers.

***Pause:***

- How readily do you intercede for others' needs, and how readily do you invite others to intercede for your needs? If there is reluctance, why might this be?
- Can you think of any examples, either from your own life or from the lives of others known to you, in which intercession has made a difference? What happened?

## WHAT: What is the biblical basis for learning to lean in?

In Mark 2:1-12 we find an example of this principle being outworked in the story of the paralysed man and his four friends.

It would perhaps be an understatement to say that life is tough for the paralysed man! Yet in this story he makes a life-changing choice. He chooses to involve the people who God has placed around him in community. He chooses to allow them to support him, uplift him and bring him to Jesus.

He makes the choice to lean in – and we can learn from his example.

It's a story that gives us three *keys* that we can use to *unlock* this principle.

- **KEY 1: We need friends who will overcome obstacles for us (Mark 2:1-4)**

  A few days later, when Jesus again entered Capernaum, the people heard that he had come home. They

> gathered in such large numbers that there was no room left, not even outside the door, and he preached the word to them. Some men came, bringing to him a paralysed man, carried by four of them. Since they could not get him to Jesus because of the crowd, they made an opening in the roof above Jesus by digging through it and then lowered the mat the man was lying on.

This story is set in Capernaum, a village on the shore of Lake Galilee where Jesus is now living, probably in Peter's house. As word spreads, a diverse crowd of people gather there, having come from far and wide – and one of them, keen to get in, is a paralysed man.

This man is experiencing a truly tough time. He would have been totally immobile, probably in pain, and largely consigned to a mat on the floor.

Without a social security system to support those who were sick or disabled, he would have been reliant on charity for his needs to be met, and he might have had to beg by the roadside or in a public place. Furthermore, most people would have assumed he was paralysed due to sin in his life, meaning he would also have been dealing with social stigma.

In other words, he is helpless, dependent and isolated, as well as paralysed. It is as much an emotional and spiritual condition as a physical one.

Yet this man has heard about Jesus. He knows that, if he can get to Jesus, Jesus can heal him. In fact, in Luke's version of this story we read that "the power of the Lord was with Jesus to heal the sick."[18]

So the man makes a decision. He decides to lean in on his friends, the men in his life who share his belief that Jesus can heal him, and four of them commit to carry him to Jesus. Even when they arrive to discover the crowd spilling out onto the street, the door inaccessible, they are undeterred. They will happily overcome obstacles to get their friend to Jesus.

Houses in those days usually had flat roofs, with a set of stairs running up an outside wall, allowing access to the roof for use as an additional living space. These roofs were created in layers. Timbers would be laid across the top of the house, connecting the walls, and these would then be covered by branches. A layer of thick mud would then be added, rolled and pressed, until the roof was solid and rainproof.

As they look at the house, these four friends decide to carry their paralysed friend up the outside stairs and onto the roof, where they place him to one side while they slowly start to strip away each of the layers in the roof, until there's an opening that's large enough for their friend's mat to fit through.

Can you imagine the scene inside that house?

As Jesus is preaching, the sound of digging can be heard overhead. Initially, the assembled crowd try to ignore it, but then it gets louder. They can feel the debris, dirt and dust falling onto them, so they look up, wondering what's

18. Luke 5:17

happening. Jesus joins them. Nobody can concentrate on what he is saying with such a kerfuffle going on up above.

Then, before they know it, a growing patch of bright blue sky starts piercing through the ceiling – and they watch in utter amazement, shuffling out of the way, making space, as the paralysed man is slowly lowered, a delicate balancing act, ropes undergirding his mat, onto the floor of the room.

This man, in choosing to lean in on his friends, could never have known what obstacles they would be willing to overcome in order to get him to Jesus. They were willing to break down barriers, both literally and socially. Even if it led to profound discomfort in the crowd. Even if it annoyed Peter, the likely house-owner. Even if it made them liable for the roof repairs.

All they know is that if they can get their friend to Jesus, Jesus can heal him.

***Pause:***

Are you like the paralysed man in this story, facing a seemingly intractable tough time? You may not be *physically* paralysed, but you may feel paralysed *emotionally* or *spiritually*.

Maybe you feel numb because of something that's happened to you. Maybe you know you need help, but you don't want to be a burden on others. Maybe you are struggling to connect with God, running away from him, rather than towards him.

If this is you, who are your Christian friends who you can lean on in your tough time?

Not your followers on social media. Not your virtual online "friends". But your real-life friends who will overcome obstacles to bring you before Jesus. Your friends who will help you strip back the layers, one by one, if that's what's needed to get you to Jesus. Your friends who will do whatever it takes to help you find Jesus in the midst of your mess. Your friends who you can lean in on.

Alternatively, you may identify more with the four friends in this story. Maybe you feel burdened by someone you love who is facing a tough time. Maybe you know that, if you can only get them to Jesus, Jesus can transform their situation.

If this is you, what obstacles might need to be overcome to bring your loved one into Jesus' presence?

Maybe you could intercede on their behalf, listening to what God is saying about their situation and sharing it with them. Maybe you could offer wise counsel or encouragement. Maybe you could provide practical support.

Are you someone who your friends can lean in on in a tough time?

If we want to learn to lean in during tough times, the first thing we need is friends who will overcome obstacles for us.

- **KEY 2: We need friends who are full of faith in Jesus (Mark 2:5-9)**

  When Jesus saw their faith, he said to the paralysed man, "Son, your sins are forgiven."

  Now some teachers of the law were sitting there, thinking to themselves, "Why does this fellow talk like that? He's blaspheming! Who can forgive sins but God alone?"

  Immediately Jesus knew in his spirit that this was what they were thinking in their hearts, and he said to them, "Why are you thinking these things? Which is easier: to say to this paralysed man, 'Your sins are forgiven,' or to say, 'Get up, take your mat and walk?'"

In this part of the story, it is crucial that we notice whose faith it is that Jesus sees.

Here is the paralysed man lying on a mat on the floor, surrounded by a sea of people, all craning their necks to get in on the action. The only thing in his line of sight is a great gaping hole in the ceiling above him, his four friends' faces peering tentatively over the edges, trying to make out what is happening beneath them.

Then Jesus looks down at him, looks up at his four friends, observes five men – *and sees their faith.* Jesus sees beyond the man's paralysed body. He sees beyond the damaged roof and the rubble that has cascaded into the room. He sees beyond the inconvenience caused and the interrupted proceedings. Instead, he sees five men, all of them full of faith.

And because of this, he forgives the man's sins.

He can see his need of healing, but he can also see his need for forgiveness. So he forgives him before he does anything else.

"Son," Jesus says, tenderly conveying that he belongs to God's family, "your sins are forgiven." His approach is kind; his words are without reproach. He knows this man, already feeling so stigmatised and isolated, needs affirmation, not condemnation.

Yet this simple statement riles some of the teachers of the Law seated in the room, their indignation rising at what they witness. *Who is this man, Jesus, to be saying this? How dare he claim to do something only God can do? This is blasphemy of the highest order!*

These men are religious scribes, writers with responsibility for copying God's Law; some are expert scholars; others have authority as interpreters. They all have comprehensive knowledge of what God's Law says about forgiveness of sins, so they immediately understand that Jesus is claiming to be God.

But Jesus is unfazed.

He knows what is going on in their hearts; their unspoken accusations; their hypocrisy and legalism. So, he poses a challenge. He designs it to deliberately contrast their *cynicism* with the *faith* of the paralysed man and his four friends.

"Why are you thinking these things?" he asks, and then, "Which is easier: to say to this paralysed man, 'Your sins are forgiven,' or to say, 'Get up, take your mat and walk?'"

Jesus knows that both these things require God's powerful intervention, but only one can be visibly demonstrated and proven. The five men are full of faith for both, but the cynicism of the religious leaders will not deliver either.

***Pause:***

Can you imagine how it must have felt for the paralysed man and his four friends to have their faith in Jesus publicly affirmed?

Maybe you are like them, full of faith in Jesus.

Maybe, like the paralysed man, you know that Jesus can turn around your tough time, and you feel grateful for your friends who have carried you into his presence through their prayers, believing likewise.

Maybe, like the four friends, you know he can do it for the tough times facing your friends in need.

If this is you, give thanks to God that you and your friends are full of faith.

Or maybe you find yourself relating more to the teachers of the Law – cynical, doubtful, questioning whether Jesus can really heal a friend in need, or transform a particularly tough time.

If this is you, what is driving your cynicism and doubt? Could it be the influence of our culture, where being sarcastic or witty is deemed desirable?

In this story, the paralysed man and his four friends are focused on Jesus – and full of faith. By contrast, the teachers of the Law are honing in on the rights and wrongs of the situation – and full of cynicism.

So, perhaps what matters most is who or what you are looking at? Is it Jesus? Or the situation?

Take time to shift your focus onto Jesus and ask God to fill you afresh with faith.

If we want to learn to lean in during tough times, the first two things we need are friends who will overcome obstacles for us and friends who are full of faith in Jesus.

- **KEY 3: We need Jesus, who knows our need (Mark 2:10-12)**

  "But I want you to know that the Son of Man has authority on earth to forgive sins." So he said to the man, "I tell you, get up, take your mat and go home." He got up, took his mat and walked out in

> full view of them all. This amazed everyone and they praised God, saying, "We have never seen anything like this!"

As we reach this part of the story we can sense the suspense in the room. Everyone's eyes are on Jesus. If he pronounces healing and nothing happens, he will be a proven fraud. But if the paralysed man gets up and walks, everyone will know that he is God.

So, Jesus now delivers!

"But I want you to know that the Son of Man has authority on earth to forgive sins," he says, firmly erasing all cynicism in an instant.

Then, with authority and power, he demonstrates that he is God Incarnate, the Messiah: with authority, he forgives sins; with power, he heals paralysis. There is no prayer, no incantation, no hype. Just a simple command, spoken in a way that means the man has no choice but to obey: "I tell you," Jesus says, "get up, take your mat and go home."

Jesus knows the man needs both forgiveness and healing. His heart has been healed; now his flesh can follow. He has been inwardly renewed; now it will be outwardly visible. He can also "go home" and get on with the rest of his life.

The healing is instantaneous. Without hesitation, the man stands, picks up his mat, pushes his way through the stunned onlookers, and walks out of the front door, all eyes on him. He must have been as amazed as everyone else.

His four friends up on the roof, no doubt peering over the edges of the gaping hole in the roof, witnessing what has just happened in the room below, probably bound down the outside staircase in utter wonder and awe. Can you imagine the joy and jubilation as they hug and greet their now-healed friend, on the street outside that house?

When the crowd of onlookers see this miracle, they praise God, for they have never seen anything like it.

All because this formerly-paralysed man had some friends who he knew he could lean in on, four of whom were prepared to carry him into Jesus' presence, overcoming obstacles along the way, full of faith for healing – leading to their friend having a life-changing encounter with Jesus, who knew his every need.

***Pause:***

Jesus knows your needs. He has the power and authority to transform your tough time. All he asks is that you come into his presence prepared for a life-changing encounter.

Jesus is the one who knows what needs saying, praying or doing; he will determine what will happen and in what order. Maybe he will offer you forgiveness first, healing second. Maybe he will ask you to do something seemingly impossible – the equivalent of picking up your mat and walking.

Praise Jesus for knowing your needs. Praise him for being one you can lean in on.

If we want to learn to lean in during tough times, the three things we need are friends who will overcome obstacles for us, friends who are full of faith in Jesus, and Jesus who knows our needs.

When the paralysed man reached out to his friends who believed in Jesus' power to heal, none of them could have envisaged how that day would pan out. By leaning in on his friends, their faith and their ability to carry him into Jesus' presence, his tough time was turned around and his life changed forever.

## HOW: How can we learn to lean in, in practice?

The good news is that God wants all of us to have Christian friends to lean in on when we are in a crisis. He also wants us to learn to be that sort of friend to others. It's part of God's good design.

Our faith is meant to be a corporate experience in which we meet regularly with other Christians. We are meant to worship God together, learn from the Bible together, pray for each other, support each other and bear each other's burdens.

God designed us to rejoice with each other during good times, console each other during sad times, and carry each other during tough times. He intended us for inter-dependent living. He created us with an innate need for each other.

So, what can we do, practically, to learn to lean in?

- **Learn to lean in – by seeking to serve your local Christian community**

For over 2,000 years, and for all its flaws, being in fellowship with other believers remains God's model for Christian community. This usually involves rooting ourselves into a local church,[19] near to where we live, so that we can discover our spiritual gifts and use them for everyone's benefit.

Whatever our Christian community looks like,[20] this is the context in which we can learn to serve and be served; to lean in and be leant on.

Unfortunately, our faith is all-too-often infused by our modern-day Western culture, which idolises individualism and self-reliance. As a result, we tend to place far too much emphasis on our personal relationship with God, frequently viewing corporate worship only as a way of furthering our individual walk with God. It can make us consumers when it comes to church, extracting what we can for our own spiritual gain, rather than cultivating an attitude that seeks first to serve.

But genuine Christian community is meant to be completely counter-cultural. It's meant to be hallmarked, first and foremost, by servant-heartedness. It's why Galatians 5:13 encourages us to "serve one another humbly in love", and Philippians 2:3-4 urges us to "in humility value others above yourselves, not looking to your own interests but each of you to the interests of the others".

19. If you have had a bad experience of local church, please seek to forgive and, if possible, to reconcile with the offending person. Then find an alternative local church, but don't forsake the body of Christ.
20. For example, you may have Christian friends who go to different churches.

The more we learn to serve our fellow believers, the more we will learn how to lean in.

- **Learn to lean in – by making meaningful real-life friends**

We are not talking here about virtual friends in online forums and on social media platforms, where connections are superficial, lacking in emotional depth, void of the nuance of face-to-face interactions.

We are also not talking about virtual church services which, while offering comfort and convenience, do not fulfil the clarion call of Hebrews 10:25 about "not giving up meeting together, as some are in the habit of doing".

We are talking about genuine real-life friends – Jesus' equivalent of Peter, James and John. The handful of believers who are willing to love us at our worst, as well as our best; to share in our sorrows, as well as our joys. The ones who we can lean in on when life turns tough, knowing they will pray with us, pray for us, and provide us with practical and spiritual support. The ones with whom we have been, and continue to be, vulnerable.

Even with two or three meaningful real-life Christian friends,[21] we will have enough to learn how to lean in.

- **Learn to lean in – by praying for others and asking for prayer**

21. For those who don't find this easy, Friendship Lab provides training and resources: www.friendshiplab.org, accessed 3 November 2025.

Corporate prayer meetings are arguably one of the most strategically important events in the local church. They allow us to intercede for all sorts of needs. They teach us how those needs are communicated. They model for us how we are meant to lean in on Jesus and each other.

Modern technology also offers multiple methods that enable us to invite people to pray with us and to persevere in praying for as long as is needed, many of which are demonstrated in the stories in *Light Through the Cracks.*

The more we learn to intercede for others, the more we will learn how to lean in on them when we need them to intercede for us.

***Pause:***

- In what ways are you serving in your local Christian community, and how is this teaching you to lean in on those who are in it?
- Can you think of an example of anyone in a tough time, who learnt to lean in on their Christian community and encountered God as a result?

## Digging Deeper

Now could be a good time to practise learning to lean in on others.

### Exercise

- Invite the Holy Spirit to guide your thoughts.
- Consider your tough time. What facts are you facing? What truth are you choosing?[22]
- Ask God to give you the names of two or three Christian friends who would be willing to pray for you. Then call or email each of them, asking them to pray for you and asking how you can pray for them.
- Be specific. If you are going through a tough time, tell them what facts you are facing and what truth you are choosing, plus any other needs.
- Also, be honourable. Take time to pray for whatever needs they share with you.

If you are doing this exercise with others, you could share your prayer needs verbally, in twos or threes, and then pray together over what has been shared. You could also share how it feels to lean in on, and be leant on by, each other.

## Worship Songs

- "Brother, Let Me Be Your Servant" by Richard Gillard.
- "Where Two Or Three" by Graham Kendrick.

## Further Reading

- *Unlocking the Miraculous Through Faith and Prayer* by Daniel Kolenda.

22. This concept is covered in Chapter 1, "Listen".

## Additional questions for small groups

- How do we currently support each other, prayerfully, emotionally and practically? In what ways does this differ, if at all, when one of us is going through a tough time?
- What is this teaching us about leaning in on Jesus and each other?

CHAPTER 3

# Let Go

## When life turns tough, what spiritual hindrances might need addressing?

*"For we live by faith, not by sight."*
(2 Corinthians 5:7)

### Introduction

When life turns tough, we face a choice.

Will we let God reveal, and deal with, any spiritual hindrances?

Will we live by *sight*, simply assuming that the circumstances of our tough time should be taken at face value? Or will we live by *faith*, asking God to disclose whether there are any spiritual dynamics that might be getting in the way, and then letting him show us how to deal with them?

For this to happen, we have to choose to be open to the possibility of letting go of invisible spiritual baggage – and that choice starts with exercising godly discernment.

## WHERE: Where does the principle of learning to let go originate?

In some (but not all) of the healing[23] stories in *Light Through the Cracks*, God reveals that there are invisible spiritual hindrances at work, which are exacerbating the tough times for the people involved. For some of them, it feels as though their prayers are hitting an invisible ceiling and bouncing back unanswered, until God shows them what is happening in the spiritual realm.

In the stories where this applies, God also shows those involved what they need to do to let go of those hindrances – and then, when they do so, it leads to breakthrough.

Common examples of these types of hindrances include sin that needs to be confessed; forgiveness that needs to be extended to someone who has caused hurt or wrong; or disobedience, where God has asked for something to be done and it simply needs doing.

Rarer examples include things like curses, occult activity, generational iniquity, demonic oppression, or ungodly soul ties – which I sadly do not have time to unpack in detail within the confines of this book.[24]

I want to be clear that this principle is *not* universal, but it *is* quite common, which is why I am including it. I also

23. *Light Through the Cracks* contains stories that reflect various kinds of miracles, not just healing miracles.
24. For more on this, please see the further reading suggestions at the end of this chapter, or search online for Ellel Ministries.

want to be clear that it is *not* about looking for things that are simply *not* there, as this can be profoundly unhelpful. (Perhaps we need a sign that says, "No fishing!") However, if there *are* things there, it can be wise to let God bring them to the surface, so that we can address them with him – and then let go of them. Our role is simply to be alert and open to God's supernatural revelation, for example, through spiritual discernment or words of knowledge.

As Deuteronomy 29:29 says, "The secret things belong to the LORD our God, but the things revealed belong to us and to our children forever." In other words, some things are for only God to know, while other things are for him to reveal to us, including anything that we need to let go of in our tough times.

For the stories where this principle applies, what unites them is that the removal of these hindrances leads to a shift change in the prayers of the people involved, and the tough times turning around.

In "Power In the Name of Jesus", Chapter 3 of *Light Through the Cracks*, we read Karen's story.

When Karen receives a diagnosis of stomach cancer, she is convinced it is not of God and encourages her prayer supporters to lean in and listen to God on her behalf.

As a result, God gives three different people, in three different countries, who don't know each other, the exact same word of knowledge. Through them, God reveals to Karen that her cancer has been caused by an occultic curse from a witchdoctor, dating back to a time when she had lived in an African nation.

By bringing it into the open, God enables Karen to deal with this invisible hidden hindrance to her healing, including forgiving the man in question and cutting off the demonic power behind his curse.

***Pause:***

- Can you think of a tough time, either in your own experience or that of someone known to you, in which a spiritual hindrance had to be addressed? How did God bring it into the open, and how was it dealt with?

## WHY: Why do we need to learn to let go?

I would like to suggest there are four reasons why we need to learn to let go.

- **Firstly, we need to learn to let go – because sin and holiness can't coexist**

Ever since the Garden of Eden, sin has been part of the human condition, and none of us is exempt. As Romans 3:23 says, "For *all* have sinned and fall short of the glory of God" (italics mine). Put simply, our sin acts as a barrier between us and God. It makes us unworthy in his sight. It prevents us from coming into his presence. It dishonours his holiness.

In Leviticus 11:44 God declares, "I am the LORD your God; consecrate yourselves and be holy, because I am holy." This is reiterated in 1 Peter 1:15, which urges, "But just as he who called you is holy, so be holy in all you do." Yet God's holiness is an impossible standard for us to attain – which is why we need a Saviour.

Jesus lived a sinless life and died on our behalf, a perfect sacrifice for our sins. Three days later he rose again, conquering sin once and for all. Now, when we sin, "If we confess our sins, he [God] is faithful and just and will forgive us our sins and purify us from all unrighteousness."[25] Without Jesus, we would not be able to let go of our sins. But Jesus' blood, shed for us, covers our guilt, meaning we can "purify ourselves from everything that contaminates body and spirit, perfecting holiness out of reverence for God."[26]

If we don't let go of our sin, it can act as a spiritual hindrance between us and God, causing our prayers to hit an invisible ceiling. As David declares in Psalm 66:18, "If I had cherished sin in my heart, the Lord would not have listened."

David knows this first hand. Early in his reign, rather than going off to war to lead his men in battle, he stays behind at home. From the balcony of his palace, he sees a beautiful woman bathing, lusts after her, commits adultery with her, gets her pregnant, tries to get her husband to sleep with her to cover it up, has him murdered when he won't, and then takes his wife as his own – following which she bears him a son.

25. 1 John 1:9
26. 2 Corinthians 7:1

"But the thing David had done displeased the LORD," says 2 Samuel 11:27, in a somewhat ironic understatement!

It is only when God sends the prophet Nathan to rebuke him, that David wakes up to the devastating consequences of what he has done. "I have sinned against the LORD," he says in 2 Samuel 12:13-14. "The LORD has taken away your sin," Nathan replies. "You are not going to die. But because by doing this you have shown utter contempt for the LORD, the son born to you will die." And this is what happens, in one of the toughest times of his life.

David, in response, writes Psalm 51, beautifully expressing his desire to let go of his sin: "Create in me a pure heart, O God," he says, "and renew a steadfast spirit within me. Do not cast me from your presence or take your Holy Spirit from me."

As we learn to let go, we need to be open to God revealing where our sin is acting as a hindrance, and then "throw off everything that hinders and the sin that so easily entangles"[27] – by confessing, repenting and letting it go.

***Pause:***

Take a moment to invite God to reveal any areas of your life where you have sinned in your thoughts, words or actions, or in things you have failed to do or say. With each thing God highlights: confess, repent, let it go, and receive God's forgiveness.[28]

27. Hebrews 12:1
28. If it helps, visualise the cross of Jesus in your mind's eye, see yourself walking up to it and placing your sin there, then walking away and leaving it behind. See also the exercise at the end of this chapter.

- **Secondly, we need to learn to let go – because forgiveness is foundational for our relationships**

Have you ever noticed how, in the Scriptures, forgiveness is often conditional? "When you stand praying," Jesus tells his disciples in Mark 11:25, "if you hold anything against anyone, forgive them, so that your Father in heaven may forgive you your sins."

The conclusion is clear: if we want God to forgive us, we need first to forgive others.

If we are harbouring unforgiveness towards anyone who has hurt or wronged us, it will fester in our hearts and God won't be able to forgive us for our own sins, unless and until we let it go. Yet God longs to forgive us. As Ephesians 4:32 says, "Be kind and compassionate to one another, forgiving each other, just as in Christ God forgave you."

It can sometimes be painful and difficult to forgive, making it not so much an instantaneous decision as a process that can take a long time. But if we don't let go of any grievances that have happened to us, our unforgiveness can become like a tap root, leading to resentment, disillusionment, cynicism, anger and all sorts of other ugly emotions embittering our hearts.

Our unforgiveness can also, sometimes, be the *cause* of our tough times. It is arguably one of the principal spiritual hindrances to God being able to turn things around, and we must learn to let go of it.

In "X-rays Never Lie", Chapter 2 of *Light Through the Cracks*, we read the story of Keith, who suffers an unexpected stroke at the age of sixty.

Aware that stress could have been one of the main causes of his stroke, Keith senses God prompting him to forgive two people who have caused it. One is the leader of his workplace, who has failed to address his enormous workload yet subsequently replaces him with three people. Another is the lodger in the family home, who has been draining Keith's emotional energy reserves.

Keith refuses to take offence at these people. He doesn't want it to become an invisible spiritual hindrance to healing – so he chooses to forgive them and let go of the wrong they have caused him.

***Pause:***

Take a moment to allow God to bring to mind anyone you need to forgive. This may include people whose actions and words have inadvertently hurt you, as well as those who have said or done things deliberately. With each person God highlights: forgive them, release them and ask God to bless them. Depending on the nature of the situation, you may find you need to do this more than once, on an ongoing basis.[29]

29. Remember that forgiving someone does not let them off the hook for the wrong that they have done to you. Rather, it is giving them to God, for him to deal with as he sees fit.

- **Thirdly, we need to learn to let go – because blessings follow obedience**

Tucked into the Old Testament is the story of Jonah, who hears the word of the LORD – but disobeys. Rather than going to the city of Nineveh with a message of repentance, he heads for the port of Tarshish and boards a boat. "Jonah ran away from the LORD," we are told in Jonah 1:3.

What follows is an incredibly tough time, involving a violent storm, rough seas, a ship in danger of being completely wrecked – and a stricken conscience. "Pick me up and throw me into the sea," Jonah tells the sailors in Jonah 1:12, "and it will become calm. I know that it is my fault that this great storm has come upon you."

God is merciful. Rather than allowing Jonah to drown, he provides a huge fish to swallow him. Three days later, it spews him out onto dry land, and God subsequently gives Jonah a second chance. This time, humbled and willing to let go of his disobedience, we read how "Jonah obeyed the word of the LORD and went to Nineveh."[30]

Disobedience is often linked to pride. It comes from an attitude that thinks we know better than God for our lives, and it damages our relationship with him. Yet he longs to bless those who obey him. As Jesus says in Luke 11:28, "Blessed rather are those who hear the word of God and obey it."

As we learn to let go, we need to recognise that disobedience can act as a powerful spiritual hindrance between us and God.

30. Jonah 3:3

In "Building on God's Grace", Chapter 7 of *Light Through the Cracks*, we read the story of St Thomas' Church.

At one point in the story, a couple called Al and Lucy are living in the St Thomas' vicarage. However, they are attending a different church, where Al is the curate.[31]

About a year before the end of his curacy, Al is considering options and successfully applies for a role in a different part of the country. Everyone is notified.

Six weeks before they are due to move, Al is attending a special service at the cathedral when he starts to feel a deep sense of unease and doubt about the pending move. Recognising that this could be a prompt from God, he and Lucy pray and seek wise counsel.

Nine days later, Al withdraws from the role.

He and Lucy both feel sure that it's the right decision, even though it leaves them with huge uncertainty. All they know is that they need to obey God's leading.

***Pause:***

Take a moment to think back to the last thing you heard God asking you to do. It might have been recently or a long time ago. How did you respond? If you were obedient, give thanks. But if you were disobedient, confess it to God. Ask him to give you a second chance. Then trust and obey what he is asking of you.

31. A curate is a trainee vicar in the Church of England.

- **Fourthly, we need to learn to let go – because we are instructed to live by faith, not sight**

In 2 Corinthians 5:7 Paul reminds us: "For we live by faith, not by sight." Yet many Christian believers don't seem to live like this. When tough times hit, their faith seems to inexplicably evaporate, only to be replaced by doubt, cynicism and unbelief. *If I've never known God to do a miracle,* they tell themselves, *then why would he do one now?* Yet this type of faulty mindset creates a profound spiritual hindrance to God being able to break in and turn things around.

After Jesus' resurrection he appears to almost all the disciples – apart from Thomas, who declares that he needs to see and touch him to believe. One week later and Jesus appears again to the disciples. This time, Thomas is there and Jesus invites him to reach out and touch him.

"Stop doubting and believe," he tells him, and immediately Thomas lets go of his scepticism. "My Lord and my God!" he cries. Then Jesus makes a statement that has echoed through the generations ever since: "Because you have seen me, you have believed," he says, but "blessed are those who have not seen and yet have believed."[32]

When we are in a tough time, we need to let go of our doubt and unbelief. If we don't, it can act as a spiritual hindrance, making it difficult for God to break into our situation. This is why James 1:6-8 cautions us: "But when you ask, you must believe and not doubt, because the one who doubts is like a wave of the sea, blown and tossed by the wind. That person

32. John 20:27-29

should not expect to receive anything from the Lord. Such a person is double-minded and unstable in all they do."

By contrast, Mark 11:23 shows what happens when doubt is banished from our minds: "If anyone says to this mountain, 'Go, throw yourself into the sea,' and does not doubt in their heart but believes that what they say will happen, it will be done for them.'"

As we learn to let go, we need to relinquish all doubt, cynicism and unbelief to stop them becoming an invisible spiritual hindrance to the turnaround we need.

In "Release From a Prison of Darkness", Chapter 10 of *Light Through the Cracks*, we read the story of Anna, a talented teenage dancer.

There are many moments in Anna's story when she feels anything but close to Jesus. Her illness goes on for so long that her faith flounders, doubt and unbelief feel very real, and she wonders whether she will ever get well.

It is only when she has a powerful encounter with the Holy Spirit that she sees how far she has drifted, returns to the Lord, and lets go of her lack of faith.

***Pause:***

Take a moment to consider the extent to which you are living by faith, or sight, at the moment. Why might this be? If you are finding it a struggle, confess any doubt, cynicism or unbelief as sin. Then ask God to give you fresh faith.

## WHAT: What is the biblical basis for learning to let go?

In Mark 6:1-6 we find an example of this principle being outworked in the story of Jesus returning to his hometown of Nazareth.

This story shows us four spiritual hindrances, all of which block Jesus from being able to do many miracles there – unlike in other places, where he performs multiple miracles. It shows us the sad consequences for people who do not learn to let go.

It's a story that gives us four *keys* that we can use to *unlock* this principle:

- **KEY 1: Taking Jesus for granted can be a hindrance (Mark 6:1-2)**

  Jesus left there and went to his hometown, accompanied by his disciples. When the Sabbath came, he began to teach in the synagogue, and many who heard him were amazed.

  "Where did this man get these things?" they asked. "What's this wisdom that has been given him? What are these remarkable miracles he is performing?"

This story is set in Jesus' hometown of Nazareth, where he grew up and where his family still lives. Built on a rocky hillside, miles from anywhere important, it's an obscure and sleepy backwater. The population is small, and it's the sort of place where everyone knows each other's business, so Jesus isn't anonymous.

Before this visit, the last time Jesus saw his family was in Capernaum, when they had travelled the forty miles from Nazareth to confront him. On that occasion[33] they had been so convinced that he was out of his mind that they had attempted (unsuccessfully) to seize him.

Because of the tensions that resulted, news of Jesus' arrival is the talk of the town: *Ooh,* they might have been thinking, *have you heard? Jesus is back and he's brought his disciples with him. Do you think there will be any drama? This I must see!*

Jesus waits for the Sabbath, the first Saturday after his arrival – and then he enters the synagogue and starts to teach the people. Perhaps unsurprisingly, many who hear him are amazed. After all, this is a typical response to Jesus' authority and wisdom.

But the difference here is that these people have known Jesus since he was a toddler. They have watched him grow up. They have seen his family through all their ups and downs. Here in Nazareth is where he used to run down the streets with his friends. It's the place where his father, Joseph, taught him the carpentry trade.

Yet, here he is, entering the synagogue, teaching them like a rabbi! And he's being accompanied by a group of students who seem to be following him wherever he goes.

33. Mark 3:20-21

They know he hasn't had a learned education, or gone to the equivalent of modern-day theological college. They know he hasn't studied under any of the great rabbis of his day, or qualified as a teacher. They know he lacks the credentials to be a rabbi.

Jesus is so familiar to them that they have always just taken him for granted. Yet, as they listen, they can't quite comprehend the wisdom in his teaching. Nor the remarkable miracles they have heard about. It leaves them feeling bewildered.

They *think* they know who he is – but they *don't actually know* who he is. For far too long, they have just taken him for granted.

***Pause:***

Have you, like the people in this story, known Jesus for a long time? Do you ever make assumptions about who he is and how he should be operating?

Maybe you feel like you're going through the motions in your relationship with Jesus. Maybe, if you're being honest, you take him for granted.

Have you ever considered that taking Jesus for granted can be a hindrance to miracles?

Maybe the Bible has become so familiar that reading it feels dull and boring. Maybe praying has become repetitive and routine. Maybe church has become something you do on Sundays, one of many activities in your busy schedule.

If this is you, pause a moment to let go of this hindrance.

Humble yourself before God. Confess that you have taken Jesus for granted. Ask for a fresh sense of amazement about your relationship with him. Wait, as God responds.

If we want to learn to let go during our tough times, the first thing we need to know is that taking Jesus for granted can be a hindrance to miracles.

- **KEY 2: Taking offence can be a hindrance (Mark 6:3)**

  "Isn't this the carpenter? Isn't this Mary's son and the brother of James, Joseph, Judas and Simon? Aren't his sisters here with us?" And they took offence at him.

In these three questions, we can sense the confusion that Jesus' teaching is generating and the offence it causes.

In their opening question they ask, "Isn't this the carpenter?" Not, "Isn't this *the son of* the carpenter?" This means they know Jesus as a carpenter in his own right, independent of Joseph, his father.

The word in the text actually describes someone involved in building. It's a word that can mean both "carpenter" and "stonemason". So it's possible that, as well as building with wood, Jesus might also have built with stone. Either way, in Jesus' era, builders[34] didn't have any status or prestige. They were menial labourers who built items such as tables, mangers, yokes for oxen and single-storey houses.

In their second question they ask, "Isn't this Mary's son?" Not, "*Joseph and* Mary's son". It's intentionally insulting, highly sarcastic, and designed to cause maximum offence.

Legally speaking, Jews would always name their men in relation to their father and, even if Joseph had died by now, this custom would still hold. So why is Joseph not mentioned? Could it be because the people of Nazareth believed Jesus was illegitimate, born out of wedlock?

Perhaps they are thinking: *Isn't he that illegitimate baby who Mary bore? Who does he think he is?* It reminds us that they have been offended by Jesus since he was in the womb.

And in their third question they ask, "Isn't he the brother of James,[35] Joseph, Judas and Simon? Aren't his sisters here with us?" For they know him in the context of his family, his siblings.

Their three questions reveal how they are wrestling between *what they think they know* and *what they are witnessing*, and the dichotomy is deeply offensive.

34. Also known as construction workers.
35. After Jesus' resurrection, his brother James became a believer. He led the church in Jerusalem and wrote the book of James in the New Testament.

He is shaming them all, acting as if he's a rabbi, when his only training has been as a carpenter, not a rabbi. He's an embarrassment, a disgrace, an offence. Not just to his family, but to his entire hometown community, especially those in the synagogue that day.

***Pause:***

Have you, like the people in this story, ever taken offence at someone?

Are you aware that when you take offence, it becomes like a bitter root on which other things grow and fester – things like anger, resentment and unforgiveness?

Taking offence is like Satan's bait. He uses it to hook you in, like a fisherman with a line. It then infects your soul and spirit – and it becomes a profound hindrance to Jesus being able to do miracles.

But he loves you too much to want you wallowing in offence – so it needs to be rooted out.

If this is you, pause a moment to let go of this hindrance.

Invite the Holy Spirit to bring to mind anyone against whom you have harboured offence. Forgive, bless and release everyone who comes to mind. Confess this as sin. Ask God to forgive you. Then wait, as he responds.

If we want to learn to let go during our tough times, the first two things we need to know are that taking Jesus for granted, and taking offence, can both be a hindrance to miracles.

- **KEY 3: Lack of honour can be a hindrance (Mark 6:4)**

> Jesus said to them, "A prophet is not without honour except in his own town, among his relatives and in his own home."

As we read this statement, we can sense Jesus' sadness about the reception he is receiving in the synagogue that day.

He is quoting a well-known proverb from that time, but it's phrased as a double negative so it might be more easily understood as, "A prophet is honoured everywhere, except in his hometown and amongst his own family." In other words, God's people tend to respect his messengers – but not the people who have known them since they were born; those who know their history, family, faults and quirks.

The meaning is clear. He is a prophet, and they are his relatives and the people of his hometown. He is amongst those who have known him his entire earthly life, but all they are doing is dishonouring him.

The concept of "honour" is frequently misunderstood in our modern-day Western culture. Put simply, it means to respect or revere someone, to value them or give them worth. It's a heart attitude, which expresses itself in actions.[36]

By contrast, Middle Eastern culture has always placed significant value on the concept of honouring people, especially within the family, something it still does today. In the Middle East, including in Israel, it is a particularly painful and humiliating experience for anyone to be dishonoured by a relative or closely connected person, let alone a group of people.

Yet this is what Jesus is facing! Instead of accepting him, these people are rejecting him. Instead of honouring him, they are treating him with contempt.

It must have been so hard for him to go home.

***Pause:***

Have you, like the people in this story, ever shown a lack of honour towards anyone who you should have respected?

Are you aware that when you show a lack of honour towards a person who God asks you to honour, it opens the door to contempt, disdain and scorn, which is often followed by pride and one-upmanship?

These things can become a profound hindrance to Jesus being able to do miracles.

Maybe, like the people in this story, you have dishonoured Jesus.

36. Matthew 15:8

Or maybe you have dishonoured someone who God explicitly instructs all of us to honour – such as your parents,[37] your husband[38] or wife,[39] those who are older than you,[40] your church leaders[41] or your fellow believers.[42]

If this is you, pause a moment to let go of this hindrance.

Humble yourself before God. Bring each of the people before him who you know you have dishonoured. If any of them have hurt you, such that you have found it difficult to honour them, give this over to God. Ask him to help you forgive them. Ask him to heal each relationship, where possible.

Confess your sin, and ask God for his forgiveness. Ask him to fill you afresh with his Holy Spirit, so that you can see people as he sees them, worthy of honour.

If we want to learn to let go during our tough times, the first three things we need to know are that taking Jesus for granted, taking offence, and showing a lack of honour to those God calls us to honour, can all be hindrances to miracles.

37. Exodus 20:12 and Ephesians 6:2-3
38. Ephesians 5:33
39. 1 Peter 3:7
40. Leviticus 19:32
41. 1 Timothy 5:17
42. Romans 12:10

- **KEY 4: Lack of faith can be a hindrance (Mark 6:5-6)**

  He could not do any miracles there, except lay his hands on a few people who were ill and heal them. He was amazed at their lack of faith.

As we reach this stage of the story, Mark clearly wants to convey the consequences of the hindrances with which Jesus is contending. He wants us to grasp that miracles can't be guaranteed.

It's not that Jesus doesn't want to do miracles there, either on that particular day or during his stay in Nazareth. It's just that, because of the attitude towards him from the people who live there, he can only do a few – and those that he does do are the exception, not the norm.

Maybe there are a few sick people who, in their desperation for healing, seek Jesus out in secret, defying the prevailing narrative in Nazareth at that time. Maybe for everyone else, their scepticism, doubt, lack of honour or lack of faith, are acting as hindrances, so they are missing out on healing and the other miracles that could be theirs.

And Jesus, according to Mark, is "amazed" at their lack of faith.[43]

It must have been so distressing for Jesus to see such scepticism from these people who have known him his whole life; such insensitivity to the presence of God in their midst; such doubt about his power and authority. Their lack of faith was acting as a hindrance, but they simply could not see it.

43. It is interesting to note that the only other time in the Gospels when Jesus is described as "amazed" is when he encounters the faith of the centurion in Matthew 8:10 . Yet the contrast is stark. On that occasion, he is amazed at the presence of faith; on this occasion, he is amazed at the absence of faith.

***Pause:***

Have you, like the people in this story, ever lacked faith for the seemingly impossible?

Maybe you have been pressing in for a miracle that hasn't yet happened.[44] Maybe this has shaken your faith in Jesus. Maybe it has made you callous and hard-hearted. Maybe it has left you feeling disillusioned, or even outright hostile, towards God.

Or maybe you have inadvertently allowed doubt, scepticism or unbelief to influence your spirit, on the back of your lack of faith, and these have taken root within your heart.

But lack of faith can be a hindrance to Jesus being able to do miracles. "Without faith it is impossible to please God," Hebrews 11:6 says, "because anyone who comes to him must believe that he exists and that he rewards those who earnestly seek him."

So if this is you, pause a moment to let go of this hindrance.

Tell God about your tough time, and all the feelings it has generated. Confess where there has been any lack of faith. Allow God to forgive you, then forgive yourself.

44. Please remember that there is an element of mystery in how God answers our prayers, but you can trust him with the outcome, even if it's not the one you are wanting. For more on this, see Chapter 5, "Glorify".

Recognise that God doesn't want your faith to flounder. Ask him, if appropriate, for the gift of faith. Then invite the Holy Spirit to come and fill you afresh.

If we want to learn to let go during our tough times, the four things we need to know are that taking Jesus for granted, taking offence, showing a lack of honour to those God calls us to honour, and a lack of faith, can all be hindrances to miracles.

If we want to see miracles, we need to let go of these hindrances.

When Jesus headed home to Nazareth for those few days, I wonder whether he could have anticipated so many invisible spiritual barriers, blocking him from being able to do miracles in their midst. If only the people could have let go of them all, how many more tough times could have been turned around!

## HOW: How can we learn to let go in practice?

In Jeremiah 32:27 God says, "I am the Lord, the God of all mankind. Is anything too hard for me?" The question is, of course, rhetorical – and the answer is always "no". This means that our prayers can never be impeded by the degree of difficulty being faced in our tough times. However, our tough times can sometimes be compounded by invisible spiritual hindrances.

The good news is that, on the occasions when this applies, God's desire is to bring them to the surface, ready to be rooted out and removed. He does *not* want us to "go fishing" for things that aren't there, but he *does* want us to let go of anything he reveals.[45]

So, what can we do, practically, to learn to let go?

- **Learn to let go – by keeping short accounts**

Any unresolved conflict in a relationship will create distance between those involved – unless and until it's addressed. In the same way, even the smallest of sins can damage our relationship with God – unless and until we confess them and acknowledge our need of God's forgiveness.[46] In both scenarios, we need to keep short accounts.

One way to prevent sin taking root is to develop a habit of daily praying Psalm 139:23-24: "Search me, God, and know my heart; test me and know my anxious thoughts. See if there is any offensive way in me, and lead me in the way everlasting."

If the Holy Spirit convicts us of sin, we need to confess it immediately and repent. No excuses. No procrastination. Just a simple prayer, admitting our wrongdoing and asking God for grace to guard us from repeating it. If nothing else, it matters for our wellbeing: "Whoever conceals their sins does not prosper, but the one who confesses and renounces them finds mercy" (Proverbs 28:13).

45. Often, God reveals things when we learn to listen (Chapter 1) and lean in on others who will listen on our behalf (Chapter 2).
46. 1 John 1:9

Sometimes, God will reveal that we need to resolve things with those we have hurt, or forgive those who have hurt us, in order for him to forgive us.[47] Where this applies, we must not allow guilt to linger or bitterness to fester. Instead, we need to release all grudges, trusting God to "tread our sins underfoot and hurl all our iniquities into the depths of the sea."[48]

Keeping short accounts helps us develop spiritual resilience – recognising temptation, resisting sin, being responsive to God's loving correction, and preserving a clear conscience. It prepares us for tough times by teaching us how to let go.

- **Learn to let go – by developing spiritual discernment**

Spiritual discernment enables us to distinguish between good and evil, truth and falsehood, wisdom and foolishness. When cultivated wisely and well, it's one of the best ways of learning how to let go of all that is not of God. As Romans 12:2 tells us: "Do not conform to the pattern of this world, but be transformed by the renewing of your mind. Then you will be able to test and approve what God's will is – his good, pleasing and perfect will."

God gives *every* Christian some degree of discernment,[49] which grows as we mature in our faith, so that we become increasingly aware of what is contrary to God's Word, works and ways. However, he also gives some believers the *spiritual gift* of discernment of spirits, which empowers them to distinguish between angels, demons, human spirits and

47. Mark 3:20-21
48. Micah 7:19
49. 1 John 4:1

the Holy Spirit; and to others he gives the spiritual gifts of wisdom, knowledge and faith.[50]

As with all the spiritual gifts, God alone determines who gets which ones. They can't be self-selected, and they are only ever given for the common good of the body of Christ. But it is often these particular gifts – discernment of spirits, wisdom, knowledge and faith – that God uses to reveal what is going on in the spiritual realm.[51]

The more we exercise spiritual discernment – including, where applicable, through the use of these God-given gifts – the more we will learn to see things as God sees them, and let go of all that is not of him, which will prepare us well for tough times.

- **Learn to let go – by being open to God speaking through others**

Sometimes, we might be blind to the spiritual blockages that are exacerbating our tough times. We might not be able to see what God is bringing to our attention, or we might find it difficult to accept what he is revealing. In these scenarios, God might need to use other people to speak into our lives, on his behalf, to show us what needs to be brought out into the open, addressed and let go.

For this to be credible, it is vital that these people are walking closely with Jesus, are trustworthy and truthful, and are accountable to others, such as their church leaders. They also need to have our best interests at heart so that, when they share what they believe God is saying, they are doing

50. 1 Corinthians 12:7-11
51. This is expanded in Chapter 4, "Solidify".

so with pure motives.[52] And if they are exercising one of the spiritual gifts, they need to be recognised by others as carrying that gift.

For many of us, these people will be part of the Christian community that God has placed around us, but sometimes God uses complete strangers too![53]

***Pause:***

- How open are you to God revealing any spiritual hindrances that might be influencing your tough time, which you might need to let go?
- How good are you at keeping short accounts with God, and with other people?
- In what ways could you develop your spiritual discernment?

## Digging Deeper

Now could be a good time to practise letting go of one of the most common spiritual hindrances.

### Exercise

To do this exercise, you will need a large bowl plus some sticky notes or small pieces of paper, and a pen. You may also need matches.

52. Proverbs 16:2
53. "Holding onto a prophetic promise", Chapter 9 of *Light Through the Cracks* includes an example of when this happened through a stranger.

- Invite the Holy Spirit to guide your thoughts and guard your feelings.
- Close your eyes and ask God to bring to mind anyone who you need to forgive. Open your eyes and write down their names, one name per sticky note or piece of paper.
- Now do the same with any sin you have committed, for which God needs to forgive you. A single word is sufficient on each note or piece of paper, as God knows what they represent.
- Pause a moment to consider the pile of paper in front of you.
- Then take each one and rip it up, placing the ripped pieces in the bowl as you do so. As you do this, give each person and sin to God. Tell him that you forgive each person, and ask him to forgive each sin.
- Say the Lord's Prayer, focusing particularly on the lines about forgiveness.
- Now read 1 John 1:9, preferably out loud. Do you believe what it says? If not, why not?
- If it is safe to do so, and if the bowl is fireproof, you could take a match to the contents of the bowl and watch as the flames burn them up, seeing this as completely letting go. Otherwise, simply throw the ripped pieces of paper away.
- End by thanking God for what Jesus did on the cross, once and for all, to enable forgiveness. Then pray as the Holy Spirit leads you.

If you are doing this exercise with others, you could sit in a circle, place the bowl in the middle, and collate all the ripped pieces of paper in it. You could also say the Lord's Prayer together, read 1 John 1:9, and pray for each other at the end.

## Worship Songs

- "I Speak Jesus" by Charity Gayle with Abby Benton, Kristen Dutton, Raina Pratt, Carlene Prince, Jesse Reeves and Dustin Smith.
- "I'm Accepted, I'm Forgiven" by Rob Hayward.

## Further Reading

- *What Christians Should Know About the Importance of Forgiveness* by John Arnott.
- *The Bait of Satan: Living Free from the Deadly Trap of Offence* by John Bevere.
- *Blessing or Curse: You Can Choose* by Derek Prince.

### Additional questions for small groups

- How are we growing in spiritual discernment (or, for those who have it, the gift of discernment of spirits), and how are we using this to benefit each other?
- What might hold us back from accepting, and dealing with, the spiritual hindrances that God reveals to us?

CHAPTER 4

# Solidify

## When life turns tough, how good will your grasp of spiritual warfare be?

*"For though we live in the world, we do not wage war as the world does."*
(2 Corinthians 10:3)

### Introduction

When life turns tough, we face a choice.

Will we take our circumstances only as they appear in the natural realm? Or will we also recognise the spiritual dynamics at work beneath the surface? Where there is a spiritual battle going on in our situation, will we have a good grasp of the spiritual warfare required of us?

The spiritual realm is just as real as the natural realm, but we have to acknowledge it. It starts when we solidify our understanding of the spiritual battle that all of us are in, and learn how to wage spiritual warfare during our tough times.

## WHERE: Where did the idea for solidifying our understanding originate?

To "solidify" something describes the process of making something more certain or secure. It's about creating a firm foundation, developing a good grasp, or growing a robust understanding – usually of a concept, idea or theory.

It's in this sense that I am using the word "solidify" in this chapter. It's about solidifying our understanding of spiritual warfare, based on what the Bible says about it, so that we can engage effectively in the spiritual battle during tough times.

This is because, in each of the stories in *Light Through the Cracks*, God is at work in the unseen *spiritual* realm as well as the more easily observable *natural* realm and, in several of the stories, the response is spiritual warfare. It is a common theme throughout the book.

The spiritual aspects of each story are as diverse as the stories themselves. In several of the stories there is a battle between life and death over someone who is seriously unwell, in an echo of John 10:10 where Jesus says, "The thief comes only to steal and kill and destroy; I have come that they may have life, and have it to the full." Even some of the medical professionals find themselves attributing the healings to God, despite not actually believing in him, because they have no other explanation!

In one story, God sends angels – because angels and demons are real. In another, he exposes a curse – because blessings and curses are also real. And in many of the stories, we see people taking the words God has given them, picking them up, and using them as a sword. "For the word of God is alive and active," Hebrews 4:12 tells us, and "Sharper than any double-edged sword".

What matters is that the people involved are aware they are in a spiritual battle, and they have a solid understanding of spiritual warfare and the weapons at their disposal.

In "Holding Onto a Prophetic Promise", Chapter 9 of *Light Through the Cracks*, we read the story of Henrik and Inger.

After Henrik is diagnosed with blood cancer, he and his wife, Inger, choose to take hold of the prophetic word of warning and encouragement, which a stranger at church has given them, and they use it as a sword in the spiritual battle over Henrik's life.

Again and again in the tumultuous months of treatment, as they mobilise people to fast and pray, everyone unites in reminding the Enemy that God has promised them "a day of joy".

***Pause:***

- To what extent do you have an awareness of spiritual warfare? Have you ever seen the spiritual battle play out in your own experience or another person's life? How did you recognise it?

## WHY: Why do we need to solidify our understanding?

I would like to suggest three reasons why we must solidify our understanding of spiritual warfare.

- **Firstly, we need to solidify our understanding – because our battle is not against flesh and blood**

Every Christian believer is engaged in a spiritual battle, in the spiritual realm, against the devil's schemes – and it's sometimes this that is at the heart of our tough times. "For our struggle is not against flesh and blood," Ephesians 6:12 tells us, "but against the rulers, against the authorities, against the powers of this dark world and against the spiritual forces of evil in the heavenly realms."

This is hard for our 21st-century Western mindsets to grasp, where seeing is believing and anything that can't be scientifically and evidentially proven is somehow deemed to be implausible. We can try to downplay or dismiss it as nonsense, but the Bible is clear that the unseen spiritual realm is just as real as the visible natural realm; we all inhabit both realms simultaneously.

In the natural realm, a battle involves a sustained conflict between competing factions. Hostilities usually involve armed combat and are fought using military weapons, such as tanks, bombs and bullets. In a similar way, the spiritual battle involves a sustained conflict in the spiritual realm, with God's angelic heavenly armies fighting against Satan's demonic hordes of hell, using spiritual weapons such as prayer and fasting. But it is not a battle of equals; God is greater than Satan, and God always wins.

Put simply, God loves us and wants a relationship with us through Jesus. So, it's the destiny of people that lies at the heart of the spiritual battle – be it individuals, families, churches, communities and even entire nations. By contrast, Satan wants to separate and turn us away from God, and prevent us experiencing his love – so he will do all that he can to waylay God's plans and purposes for us.

In Daniel 10 we read an account that illustrates this.

Having had a God-given revelation that his nation is going to face a great war, Daniel decides to pray and fast for twenty-one days. Shortly after this timeframe ends, an angel appears and explains how God has been listening to Daniel's prayers from the moment he started praying, and how he (the angel) was despatched in response to them.

"But the prince of the Persian kingdom resisted me twenty-one days," the angel explains. "Then Michael, one of the chief princes, came to help me, because I was detained there with the king of Persia" (v.13).

In other words, as soon as Daniel began to pray about the tough time coming, a spiritual battle ensued in the heavenly realms. Not a battle against flesh and blood, but a battle against a demonic "prince". There was no doubt that God had heard Daniel's prayers. However, despite being commissioned straightaway, the angel had been detained along the way.

It's a good reminder that persevering prayer can pay off. Sometimes, there may be spiritual reasons for seeming delays, which can't be seen in the natural realm.

In "All It Takes Is One Split Second", Chapter 4 of *Light Through the Cracks*, we read the story of Adrian and Ruth, and their horrific head-on car crash.

Fairly early in the story it becomes clear that there is a spiritual battle going on over Adrian's life. More than once we are told that he might die. But we know that the fight over his life is a spiritual one and we pray accordingly.

Day and night, as God invites people to pray for Adrian and Ruth, spiritual warfare takes place in the heavenly realms on their behalf. God even wakes some people in the early hours with a prompt to pray, before releasing them to hand over to someone else.

***Pause:***

- What is your experience, if any, of spiritual warfare in tough times?
- To what extent can you relate to Daniel's experience of delays in answers to prayers?

- **Secondly, we need to solidify our understanding – because Jesus has already won the victory**

The good news about the spiritual battle is that it has already been won, once and for all, through Jesus' death and resurrection. We don't fight to achieve the victory; we fight because Jesus has already achieved the victory for us!

This means that those who place their faith in Jesus are guaranteed success in spiritual warfare; they are on the winning side. As the apostle Paul declares in 1 Corinthians 15:57, "But thanks be to God! He gives us the victory through our Lord Jesus Christ."

The Bible is full of stories of God's people conquering their enemies, triumphant and victorious, again and again. Psalm 108:13 confidently proclaims, "With God we shall gain the victory, and he will trample down our enemies." And Psalm 20:7 declares, "Some trust in chariots and some in horses, but we trust in the name of the LORD our God."

Paul, too, is confident of Jesus' victory. In Romans 8 he lists all sorts of things that could potentially separate us from God, before pronouncing in verse 37, "No, in all these things we are more than conquerors through him who loved us."

Sometimes, we simply need God to give us eyes to see that victory is ours.

There is a beautiful example of this in 2 Kings 6, where Elisha's servant gets up early one morning only to discover an enemy army surrounding the city. Terrified, he turns to Elisha. "Don't be afraid," Elisha says. "Those who are with us are more than those who are with them" (v.16).

Then Elisha prays in verse 17, "Open his eyes, LORD, so that he may see." Immediately, God opens the servant's eyes to the spiritual realm and, as he looks, he sees God's vast heavenly army on all the hills encircling the city. Assured of victory, all his fear dissipates.

No matter how big or small the fight we face, if we are in Jesus we do not need to be afraid. He that is in us is greater than the one who is in the world.[54]

In "Beautiful Inside and Out", Chapter 6 of *Light Through the Cracks*, we read the story of Rebecca and her complicated birth.

Lying helpless in a hospital bed after having an epidural, her mum, Marianne, becomes aware of heated discussions going on around her. The medical professionals are all debating the correct course of action.

As she feels fear and panic rising, she prays in Jesus' name, trusting him to intervene, and God gives her peace.

***Pause:***

- What difference does it make to you to know that Jesus' death and resurrection have already achieved victory, once and for all, in the spiritual battle?
- How would you feel if God gave you eyes to see, as Elisha's servant saw?

- **Thirdly, we need to solidify our understanding – because God has given us all the weapons we need**

Any battle in the natural realm requires a military commander to arm his soldiers with suitable weapons, such as guns, tanks

54. 1 John 4:4

and artillery. Similarly, God gives every Christian an arsenal of weapons to use in the spiritual battle, any of which will deploy his heavenly armies to where they need to be. But they are not worldly weapons.

"For though we live in the world, we do not wage war as the world does," 2 Corinthians 10:3-4 tells us. "The weapons we fight with are not the weapons of the world. On the contrary, they have divine power to demolish strongholds."

The mention here of "strongholds" is a reference to thought patterns that are built on lies, deception and negative beliefs, which act as a barrier to God's truth and hinder our relationship with God. They include arguments, philosophies, ideologies, theories and all the schemes of the world that are proud, arrogant and based on man-made reasoning. The only way to "demolish" these "strongholds" is through "divine power".

In Ephesians 6:11 and 13, we are told to "put on the full armour of God" in order to be able to stand firm *when* the day of evil comes. Such a day is not an optional extra. (It's not *if* the day of evil comes.) So, it's all about preparing for the inevitable, and "the full armour" (vv.14-17) gives us all the weapons that we need.

We start with the *belt of truth*, wrapped around our core, holding everything else in place. It requires us to centre on Jesus, who is "*the truth*",[55] through the Holy Spirit, who will "guide [us] into *all the truth*", and "speak only what he hears" from God,[56] particularly through *the truth* of God's written word in the Bible.

55. John 14:6
56. John 16:13

The *breastplate of righteousness*, worn over the chest, guards our heart and emotions. It reminds us that everyone sins and falls short of God's standards, but "righteousness is given through faith in Jesus Christ to all who believe."[57] It reminds us that Jesus, through his death and resurrection, has fulfilled God's laws on our behalf, making us holy in God's eyes.

Our *feet* are *fitted with the readiness that comes from the gospel of peace*, which means our shoes are grounded in Jesus, who is the Prince of Peace[58] and through whom we have peace.[59] It means wherever we walk, no matter what type of terrain we face, we will be prepared to share the good news of Jesus.

We hold up the *shield of faith* to "extinguish all the flaming arrows of the evil one". Faith, in this sense, is "confidence in what we hope for and assurance about what we do not see."[60] Such confident assurance protects us against the doubts, deceptions and distortions that Satan and his demonic armies may throw at us, deflecting them before they land.

The *helmet of salvation*, worn on the head, guards our mind and thoughts. It protects us from doubts about our salvation by reminding us that "God has given us eternal life, and this life is in his Son. Whoever has the Son has life."[61] It also signifies to Satan and his demonic armies that we belong to Jesus; we are marked with the seal of the Holy Spirit.[62]

Finally, we must wield the *sword of the Spirit*, which is the word of God – and the only offensive (rather than defensive)

57. Romans 3:22-23
58. Isaiah 9:6
59. John 16:33
60. Hebrews 11:1
61. 1 John 5:11-12
62. Ephesians 1:13

part of the armour. "For the word of God is alive and active," Hebrews 4:12 tells us. "Sharper than any double-edged sword, it penetrates even to dividing soul and spirit, joints and marrow; it judges the thoughts and attitudes of the heart." We wield it by declaring Scripture, in correct context,[63] or through praise and worship.[64]

In "Synchronisation Is His Watchword", Chapter 1 of *Light Through the Cracks*, I tell the story of the car accident that I was in, with my brother, while we were on holiday in the USA.

In the immediate aftermath, as news of the accident slowly reaches home in the UK, God dovetails people to be where they need to be across the two time zones.

My housemates mobilise our friends to gather and pray, together waging spiritual warfare on behalf of me and my brother, pleading with God to help us.

***Pause:***

- What strongholds are you aware of, if any, in your own thoughts, attitudes or beliefs? How might embracing God's truth help to demolish them?
- What might you need to do, practically speaking, to put on the full armour of God as a daily discipline?

63. As Jesus did in Matthew 4:1-11
64. Psalm 149:6

## WHAT: What is the biblical basis for solidifying our understanding?

In Mark 9:14-29 we find an example of this principle being outworked in the story of Jesus with a boy possessed by a demonic spirit.

In this story, the boy's condition is making life tough – not just for him but for his family. So his father faces a choice. Will he view his son's affliction solely as it appears in the natural realm? Or will he acknowledge his need of Jesus to address the spiritual dynamics of the situation?

As he solidifies his understanding of the spiritual battle, we can learn from his example.

It's a story that gives us three sets of people, three problems, and three *keys* that we can use to *unlock* this principle:

- **KEY 1: Spiritual warfare can include silencing squabbles (Mark 9:14-19a)**

The first set of people in this story are the teachers of the Law, who are embroiled in a noisy dispute with the disciples:

> When they [Peter, James, John and Jesus] came to the other disciples, they saw a large crowd around them and the teachers of the law arguing with them. As soon as all the people saw Jesus, they were overwhelmed with wonder and ran to greet him.
>
> "What are you arguing with them about?" he asked.
>
> A man in the crowd answered, "Teacher, I brought you my son, who is possessed by a spirit that has

> robbed him of speech. Whenever it seizes him, it throws him to the ground. He foams at the mouth, gnashes his teeth and becomes rigid. I asked your disciples to drive out the spirit, but they could not."
>
> "You unbelieving generation," Jesus replied, "how long shall I stay with you? How long shall I put up with you?"

This story starts with Peter, James and John coming down a mountain, with Jesus, and rejoining the other nine disciples at the bottom.

These three have just had an indescribable experience on the mountaintop – seeing Jesus transfigured, hearing God speak from heaven, and even witnessing a momentary appearance from Moses and Elijah. They are in awe, as they walk down the mountain, trying to process their shared experience.

Now, as they approach the base, they are greeted by a noisy hullabaloo – and reality returns with a bump!

It's worth noting that, in describing this reunion, Mark is keen to emphasise how *all* the disciples have *failed* to some degree. The three who have been up the mountain have been so gripped by fear that they have *failed* to fully grasp what they have just witnessed, while the other nine, left behind at the bottom, have been so caught up in arguing with the teachers of the Law that they have *failed* to notice the growing crowd of spectators, keen to listen to their altercation.

Jesus must have felt so frustrated. *Can't I even leave them for a moment?* he might have been thinking. But then the crowd see him approaching; some start running towards him; everyone's eyes pivot.

Interestingly, Mark tells us that the people are "overwhelmed with wonder" because he wants us to grasp that this is taking place in the aftermath of the transfiguration. Could it be that he is trying to convey how Jesus' clothes are still "dazzling white, whiter than anyone in the world could bleach them" (v.3); how Jesus is continuing to exude the glory of God?

For the Jews in the crowd, witnessing this, they would have immediately thought of Moses – ascending a mountain, encountering God at the top, and returning to the bottom, carrying the glory of God, his face shining brightly[65] – causing a sense of awe and wonder at what kind of "prophet" Jesus might be.

Greetings over, Jesus immediately seeks to silence the squabbling. "What are you arguing with them about?" he asks his disciples.

But before they get a chance to answer, a man in the crowd pours out a litany of woe. How he has a son who is demonised. How, in Jesus' absence up the mountain, he had hoped the disciples would help him. How they have failed to drive out the demon.

The reason this matters is because, at that time, contemporary Jewish culture believed that if a demon made someone mute, you could never learn its name – which was problematic because they assumed you had to know a demon's name in order to cast it out. It was also thought that some demons

65. Exodus 34:29-30

could be more powerful, stubborn or intimidating than others – and this might be one of them.

As a result of this, the teachers of the Law, in their pride and arrogance, have pitched in to criticise the disciples' incompetence, humiliating them in front of the crowd. In response, the crestfallen disciples have tried to defend themselves. And the result is raised voices, each side arguing their case.

"You unbelieving generation," Jesus declares, utterly exasperated at everyone's unbelief. "How long shall I stay with you?" he adds. "How long shall I put up with you?"

Immediately, the bickering stops; the squabbling is silenced. The teachers of the Law, who are so against Jesus and his disciples, shut up.

***Pause:***

Maybe, like the teachers of the Law in this story, you are embroiled in an argument with someone or, like the crowd, you are looking on at other people arguing – and Jesus is nowhere to be seen.

Now solidify your understanding of the spiritual warfare involved.

Consider how Satan delights in dissension and division; how he loves to stoke up disputes; how happy he is when we argue. Consider how it happens in households when family relationships break down;

in churches when congregations split; in nations when elections separate voters. Maybe you can relate to one or more of these scenarios.

Consider how, when Jesus is absent, there is heightened vulnerability. Yet, as soon as he appears on the scene, he can silence squabbles in an instant because he carries God's authority.

Take a moment to invite Jesus to be present in the midst of any disputes taking place in your tough time. Pause to forgive everyone involved in them. Confess your part, repent and accept God's forgiveness.

Then invite the Holy Spirit to come and fill you afresh, giving you the same authority as Jesus had, so that you can speak the word of God in ways that will silence squabbles that have been stoked up by Satan.

If this raises issues for you, which feel too large to handle alone, it might be wise to seek help from a trustworthy member of your local Christian community[66] who understands these things.

If we want to solidify our understanding of the spiritual battle during our tough times, the first thing we need to grasp is that spiritual warfare can include silencing squabbles that have been stoked up by Satan.

66. The concept of "local Christian community" is unpacked in Chapter 2, "Lean In".

- **KEY 2: Spiritual warfare can include deliverance from demons (Mark 9:19b-27)**

The second set of people in this story are the father and son, who are desperate for their tough time to be turned around:

> "Bring the boy to me."
>
> So they brought him. When the spirit saw Jesus, it immediately threw the boy into a convulsion. He fell to the ground and rolled around, foaming at the mouth.
>
> Jesus asked the boy's father, "How long has he been like this?"
>
> "From childhood," he answered. "It has often thrown him into fire or water to kill him. But if you can do anything, take pity on us and help us."
>
> "'If you can'?" said Jesus. "Everything is possible for one who believes."
>
> Immediately the boy's father exclaimed, "I do believe; help me overcome my unbelief!"
>
> When Jesus saw that a crowd was running to the scene, he rebuked the impure spirit. "You deaf and mute spirit," he said, "I command you, come out of him and never enter him again."
>
> The spirit shrieked, convulsed him violently and came out. The boy looked so much like a corpse that many said, "He's dead." But Jesus took him by the hand and lifted him to his feet, and he stood up.

As soon as Jesus asks for the boy to be brought to him, knowing its time is almost up, the demon has a spiritual stand-off with Jesus. It throws the boy into a convulsion, flinging him onto the ground, goading Jesus to respond. In an act of defiance, it makes it clear that it won't be going without a fight, and it fully intends to cause the boy as much harm as possible before it gets evicted.

It's heart-breaking to consider the harmful symptoms that this demon has been causing this boy "since childhood". Not only has it robbed him of speech, but it seizes him and throws him down to the ground. It makes him foam at the mouth, gnash his teeth and become rigid.[67] It also casts him into fire or water to try and kill him.

It has put his son into so many life-threatening situations, on so many occasions, that this father feels utterly exhausted. He's had to do more rescue operations than he can count, constantly pulling his son out of danger. It's left him feeling physically and emotionally spent.

Yet he knows there's a spiritual solution. He knows there's a demon causing it all. He knows because he's solidified his understanding of the spiritual dynamics. And he knows that only Jesus can save his son.

But this man's faith has been badly battered.

Having brought his son to the disciples for their assistance, he's instead been met by ineptitude – and then watched on, helplessly, as they and the teachers of the Law have

67. Many today would regard these symptoms as evidence of epilepsy. Whether caused by a demon or caused by epilepsy, Jesus' desire is to bring healing. He can discern what is causing the symptoms and deal with them accordingly.

vociferously debated some specific legal arguments, oblivious to his son's distress.

By the time Jesus appears on the scene, he's feeling dejected and despondent. "But if you can do anything," he pleads, his lack of faith undisguised, "take pity on us and help us."

"'*If* you can'?" Jesus queries, before adding, "Everything is possible for one who believes" (italics mine).

Everything is possible. Not just *one* thing, or *a few* things, but *every*thing. And the only prerequisite is belief. He simply has to believe.

From somewhere deep within his being, the father musters up the courage to overcome his feelings and confess his faith. "I *do* believe," he declares (italics mine). "Help me overcome my unbelief!"

Instantly, a crowd comes running to the scene, ever voyeuristic, keen to be right at the heart of the drama. But Jesus doesn't do miracles for the entertainment of the watching public; he only ever does them out of care and compassion for the one in need, and this father and son are no exception.

With power and authority he addresses the demon, rebukes it and commands it to leave, never to return. In calling it out as a "deaf and mute" spirit, he is making it clear that it's a separate spiritual entity and not an integral part of the boy. He is also demonstrating that it doesn't need a name; that labelling its attributes is enough to force it to yield.

Immediately, confronted with the presence, power and authority of Jesus, the demon obeys. It has no choice. It has to submit to God in Jesus. So it shrieks, shakes and flees.

What a spectacle for the watching public! "He's dead," they declare, as the boy lies motionless, there at the base of the mountain. But Jesus knows otherwise. He knows this boy needs a little bit of assistance. After all, that demon had been there since childhood, so maybe the boy needs reminding how to stand unaided.

Reaching out, Jesus takes him by the hand and lifts him to his feet. Everyone can see that he has been healed and restored; delivered and released; set free from all the demonic strongholds that have kept him bound for years.

I imagine the father, grinning with delight, tears of joy streaming down his face. And I picture his son slowly starting to speak, sing, laugh and discover his voice again. All because he had solidified his understanding of the spiritual dynamics involved in his son's condition – and he knew that demonic deliverance was required.

***Pause:***

Maybe, like this boy, your tough time has been going on for many years. It's been in your life for so long that you've simply got used to all the dynamics it brings with it. It's become so familiar that it feels like it's just how things will always be.

Or maybe, like this father, you've been battling with a loved one's tough time, on their behalf, for such a long time that you feel completely spent; physically and emotionally exhausted.

Now solidify your understanding of the spiritual warfare involved.

Consider how Satan delights in deception. Consider how he wants you thinking your situation can't be altered, rather than reveal (if applicable) the demon at its root. Consider how he wants everyone within the sphere of influence of a demon to be ground down and exhausted.

Consider how Jesus applies discernment to get to the root of a problem, differentiating between natural and spiritual causes. Consider how everything is possible for the one who believes in Jesus. Consider how demons have to flee from the presence of Jesus.

Take a moment to invite Jesus into your tough time. Ask him to apply his discernment to reveal whether there are any demonic aspects, or other spiritual dynamics, which you have not previously considered. Ask him to set you free from all of Satan's tactics, and then stand firm in your freedom.

If appropriate, commit to seeking specialist help from a reputable deliverance ministry.[68]

If we want to solidify our understanding of the spiritual battle during our tough times, the first two things we need to grasp are that spiritual warfare can include silencing squabbles that have been stoked up by Satan, and deliverance from demons.

68. For example: Ellel Ministries: https://ellel.uk/, accessed 6 November 2025; Freedom in Christ Ministries: https://www.ficm.org.uk/, accessed 6 November 2025; Wholeness Through Christ Ministries: https://wholenessthroughchrist.org.uk/, accessed 6 November 2025.

- **KEY 3: Spiritual warfare can include learning lessons (Mark 9:28-29)**

The third set of people in this story are the disciples, who are feeling utterly despondent:

> After Jesus had gone indoors, his disciples asked him privately, "Why couldn't we drive it out?"
>
> He replied, "This kind can come out only by prayer."[69]

The disciples must have felt like such failures. Not just the embarrassment of being unable to drive out the demon and the humiliating public criticism from the teachers of the Law, but also the shame of letting the side down during Jesus' brief absence.

It shouldn't have been like this! It was only recently[70] that Jesus called all twelve of them, commissioned them to go out in pairs, and gave them authority over demonic spirits. Up until now, they have had success in driving out demons, anointing sick people with oil and healing them. But something about today has been different. The demon today just wasn't going to budge.

Keen to learn lessons from their mistakes, they come humbly to Jesus, to ask him privately what went wrong. They want to do better next time, to develop a better track record. They know they need his advice.

"Why, Jesus?" they ask. "Why couldn't we drive out that demon?" And Jesus' answer comes straightaway. "This kind comes out only by prayer,"[71] he says.

69. Some manuscripts add "and fasting".
70. Mark 6:7-13
71. Some manuscripts add "and fasting".

Yet there is no note in the text of Jesus praying! So, why does he give the disciples this advice? The implication seems to be that prayer is integral to Jesus' lifestyle, so he's constantly connected to God's presence and power. But this isn't the case for the disciples.

Perhaps they failed to drive out the demon because they failed to pray; they failed to rely on God; they failed to press in for his presence and power. Perhaps they failed because they were too self-reliant, thinking they could do it in their own strength. And perhaps the lesson to be learnt is the vital role of prayer in plugging them into God's presence and power.

***Pause:***

Maybe, like the disciples, you feel despondent because you've failed in some way. Maybe you've been humiliated or criticised unfairly. Maybe you've let down someone you love. Maybe you've been too self-reliant. Maybe you've been struggling to pray and fast.

Now solidify your understanding of the spiritual warfare involved.

Consider how Satan loves to condemn our mistakes, rubbing in our guilt and shame. But consider, also, how Jesus can help us learn lessons from our mistakes, desiring us to do better the next time.

Take a moment to come humbly before Jesus, and ask him privately what has gone wrong in your tough time. Listen as he tells you. Ask for his help to pray more earnestly (and fast more regularly, if applicable) and invite the Holy Spirit to fill you afresh with God's presence and power.

If we want to solidify our understanding of the spiritual battle during our tough times, the three things we need to grasp are that spiritual warfare can include: silencing squabbles that have been stoked up by Satan; deliverance from demons; and learning lessons when we get things wrong.

When the father set out to find Jesus that day, he knew that Jesus had God's power and authority to cast out the demon behind his son's symptoms. He had made the life-changing choice to solidify his understanding of the spiritual battle that was raging – and it was this that ultimately transformed their tough time.

## HOW: How can we solidify our understanding in practice?

The good news is that we can continually solidify our understanding of how to wage spiritual warfare. The more we grow in knowledge of the spiritual realm, the more we can put our understanding into practice, and the easier it will be to use our spiritual weapons when tough times come.

So, what can we do, practically, to solidify our understanding of the spiritual battle?

- **Solidify your understanding – by getting to know your army commander**

In Joshua 5:13-15 the "commander of the army of the LORD" appears to Joshua, holding a drawn sword in his hand. Joshua is so overcome with reverence and awe that he falls face down on the ground. This man tells Joshua to take off his sandals, "for the place where you are standing is holy", he says, in an echo of Moses' encounter at the burning bush,[72] thus implying that the "commander of the army of the LORD" is Jesus, God in visible human form.

As commander of the army of the LORD, Jesus leads both the *heavenly* army of holy angels and the *earthly* army of prayer warriors. He wants you to choose his side in the spiritual battle, to be a willing soldier within his troops. He wants to go before you, drawn sword in his hand, to lead the spiritual fight – against Satan, sin, the world and the flesh.

If you put your faith in Jesus, he will make your identity secure as a beloved child of God. He will also give you the authority, power and weapons to be victorious in spiritual warfare. "In this world you will have trouble," he says. "But take heart! I have overcome the world."[73] "For everyone born of God overcomes the world. This is the victory that has overcome the world, even our faith."[74]

The best way to solidify your understanding of the "commander of the army of the LORD" is to trust and obey his instructions in matters of spiritual warfare.[75]

- **Solidify your understanding – by being alert to how your enemy works**

72. Exodus 3:5
73. John 16:33
74. 1 John 5:4
75. Chapter 1, "Listen", unpacks how we can hear those instructions.

Satan is your adversary in the spiritual battle, and the battlefield is your mind – where he loves to wage war through accusation, deception and temptation. If he can arouse a sense of fear, guilt or shame, his job is done. In fact, he will stop at nothing to rob you of your joy, hope and peace – which is why, in describing him, John 10:10 says, "The *thief* comes *only* to steal and kill and destroy" (italics mine).

He particularly enjoys making you doubt God's truth by telling you lies and convincing you to believe him instead, which leads you astray and separates you from God. It's a ploy he's been employing ever since the Garden of Eden – when he subtly twisted God's words by suggesting to Eve that God was withholding something good from her and Adam, and that eating the forbidden fruit would not lead to death in the way that God had said.[76]

Both Adam and Eve believed Satan's lie, rather than God's truth, and it's a tactic that your Enemy still uses today. But you can overcome this type of attack by holding fast to God and the truth of his word. As Isaiah 40:8 says, "The grass withers and the flowers fall, but the word of our God endures for ever."

It is essential that you are attentive! Don't let Satan catch you off-guard and ensnare you. For example, be aware he will twist and misinterpret the Scriptures, as he did with Jesus in the wilderness.[77] He will steal your time and attention with innocuous distractions, such as busyness, entertainment or pleasure. He will plant seeds of doubt about God's goodness. He will exploit your pain or suffering to make you question

76. Genesis 3:4-5
77. Matthew 4:1-11

God's care. He will puff you up with pride, so you arrogantly think you can live life without God. He will fill you with fear about concerns that are in God's control. He will cause inexplicable conflict in your relationships. He will tempt you into immorality. Whatever he does, he will do whatever he can to disarm you!

What you don't want is to be easy prey for Satan – or his demonic hordes – which can happen when you choose to sin or deliberately disobey God.[78] "Be alert and of sober mind," we read in 1 Peter 5:8-9. "Your enemy the devil prowls around like a roaring lion looking for someone to devour. Resist him, standing firm in the faith." James 4:7 emphasises this, saying, "Submit yourselves, then, to God. Resist the devil, and he will flee from you."

The message is clear. Be alert. Be clear-headed. Stand firm in your faith. Submit to God. Resist the Enemy. "Take captive every thought to make it obedient to Christ."[79] "Do not give the devil a foothold."[80]

- **Solidify your understanding – by using all the spiritual weapons at your disposal**

Start by deciding whose side you are on! The winner of the war has already been determined – because of Jesus' victory at the cross. This means that all of Jesus' followers can fight the spiritual battle *from* a place of victory, "strong in the Lord and in his mighty power."[81]

78. See Chapter 3, "Let Go", for more on this.
79. 2 Corinthians 10:5
80. Ephesians 4:27
81. Ephesians 6:10

Next, you need to put on your *full* spiritual armour, as described earlier in this chapter. God has designed it to provide you with *all* the weapons you need, both offensive and defensive, so you can't be selective about which pieces you want to wear. You must put it on *in full*!

You also can't be selective about which soldiers you stand alongside, because God has designed the armour to be worn in the "phalanx" formation, to ensure that everyone's backs are protected. This involves infantry foot soldiers standing shoulder to shoulder, densely packed, armed with large head-to-toe shields and either spears or swords, together creating a formidable wall, both offensively and defensively. It is one of the many reasons why you need to be in Christian community[82] – to wage spiritual warfare together.

From this place, "you can take your *stand* against the devil's schemes", "*stand* your ground" when the day of evil comes, "after you have done everything, to *stand*", and then to "*stand* firm"[83] (italics mine). There is no excuse for not having a firm footing!

One area in which you can stand firm is in the authority you have in Jesus. This includes authority to overthrow the Enemy's power: "I have given you authority," he says in Luke 10:19, "to trample on snakes and scorpions and to overcome all the power of the enemy; nothing will harm you." It also includes authority to usher in God's power: "You may ask me for anything in my name," he says in John 14:14, "and I will do it."

82. See Chapter 2, "Lean In", for more on this.
83. Ephesians 6:11-14

Call on the name of Jesus. Memorise and declare the Scriptures. Praise and worship. Fast and pray. Cultivate an attitude of gratitude. Break bread and drink wine in memory of Jesus' sacrifice. Keep reminding the Enemy that he has been defeated.[84]

As Psalm 91:4-5 proclaims: "He will cover you with his feathers, and under his wings you will find refuge; his faithfulness will be your shield and rampart. You will not fear the terror of night, nor the arrow that flies by day."

***Pause:***

- What has this section taught, or reminded, you about the reality of the spiritual battle?
- How alert are you to the tactics of the Enemy in your life, and how are you using the spiritual weapons of warfare to defeat him?

## Digging Deeper

Now could be a good time to practise solidifying your understanding of spiritual warfare.

### Exercise

To do this exercise you will need to search online for an image of "phalanx formation". You will also need your Bible, plus bread and wine.

84. We don't need to be afraid of the Enemy's tactics, but it's good to be aware of them. What matters is that we live in the reality of the victory that Jesus won for us at the cross.

- Invite the Holy Spirit to come and be present.
- Read Ephesians 6:10-20, slowly and out loud. As you read about each item of armour, pause to put it on. For example, with the belt of truth, use your hands to fasten it around your waist. Or with the helmet of salvation, pick it up with your hands and place it on your head.
- When you are wearing the whole armour, give thanks to God for it.
- Now consider your back, which is exposed, and look at the image of "phalanx formation". Ask God to bring to mind the people with whom you can stand in this formation.[85]
- Pause and consider. Why has God designed it this way? How does this formation protect you?
- Take time to pray for the people who are in "phalanx formation" with you. How can you cover their backs in prayer? How can they do likewise for you?[86]
- End by reading 1 Corinthians 11:23-26, slowly and out loud. As you do so, take the bread and break it; then the wine and pour it. Remind yourself that Jesus has already achieved the victory, once and for all, through what he achieved on the cross. Thank God that the spiritual battle has already been won.

If you are doing this exercise with others, you could try to act out the "phalanx formation" by standing together in a line (or in rows behind each other, if the group is big enough).

85. There is more on this in Chapter 2, "Lean In".
86. If appropriate, reach out and ask them, after you have done this exercise.

While you are doing this, you could discuss how it feels and talk through how you could work together to strengthen the formation between you.

## Worship Songs

- "In Heavenly Armour" by Jamie Owens-Collins.
- "Battle Belongs" by Phil Wickham and Brian Johnson.

## Further Reading

- *Victory Over the Darkness* by Neil T. Anderson.
- *Spiritual Warfare: How to Disarm the Enemy and Administer the Victory of Jesus* by Derek Prince

### Additional questions for small groups

- What experience do we have, between us, of spiritual warfare?
- How could we solidify our understanding of the spiritual battle, especially if one or more of us are going through a tough time at the moment? What could we do to wage spiritual warfare on their behalf?

CHAPTER 5

# Glorify

## When life turns tough, will you give God the glory no matter what?

*"I will praise you, Lord my God, with all my heart; I will glorify your name forever."*

(Psalm 86:12)

### Introduction

When life turns tough, we face a choice.

Will we give God the glory during our tough time, regardless of how it is unfolding? Will we give him the glory at the end of our tough time, irrespective of the eventual outcome? Or will we only glorify him if things turn out the way we want?

Glorifying God is not an optional extra. We have to be intentional about it, both during and after our tough times – and it starts when we choose to focus on God, for who he is, more than what he is doing; when we look first to his face, then to his hand.

## WHERE: Where did the idea for glorifying God originate?

To "glorify" describes the act of honouring, praising or worshipping someone or something, in ways that give importance or significance to that person or object. In today's culture, it's a word that's often associated with the idolisation of famous musicians or iconic sports stars.

In the Old Testament, the word "glory" stems from a Hebrew word meaning "weight, splendour or honour", and in the New Testament it comes from a Greek word meaning "splendour, honour or magnificence". When combined, these words convey the sense that, when we "glorify" God, we are acknowledging the radiance of his splendour; we are giving him all the honour and praise that he is due.

It's in this sense that I am using the word "glorify" in this chapter. I am trying to convey how we are called to glorify God for his faithfulness, his goodness and all his other attributes. We are called to honour and praise him, even when our tough times are not panning out as we had hoped, and even if the eventual outcome is not the one we would have wanted. We are called to glorify him, simply because he is God.

It's a common theme throughout my book *Light Through the Cracks.* Even in the stories that don't have happily-ever-after endings. Even in the midst of messy situations, when the pain is raw and real. Even when unexpected curveballs are thrown in for good measure. Why? Because God is still sovereign; he still breaks into tough times; and he still deserves to be glorified.

The people in the stories glorify God in a variety of ways. They cannot help but testify to what God has done. Some of them express profound gratitude, praise and thankfulness. Others fall before him in worship and surrender. But what unites them is that, irrespective of what is happening in the midst of the mess, and no matter how things eventually pan out, all these people choose to glorify God.

In "Hard Pressed But Not Crushed", Chapter 5 of *Light Through the Cracks*, we read the story of Jackie and her baby twins who are born extremely prematurely.

As the babies fight for life in the weeks following birth, we are taken on an emotional rollercoaster ride. Yet throughout the highs, the lows and everything in between, and even when the story includes harrowing and upsetting aspects, we see Jackie consistently giving glory to God.

She glorifies him in the way she frames her prayer updates, regularly encouraging her prayer supporters to give thanks, as well as to continue interceding. She does it through worship, with the lyrics of a specific song taking on special meaning. And she does it in the way she witnesses to the medical professionals.

***Pause:***

- Can you recall a tough time, either from your own experience or that of someone else, where a choice was made to glorify God? What did it involve?

## WHY: Why do we need to glorify God no matter what?

I would like to suggest there are three reasons why we need to glorify God no matter what.

- **Firstly, we need to glorify God – because he alone is worthy to be glorified**

When it comes to describing who God is, there aren't enough words to capture all his characteristics. Yet it's these attributes that make him worthy to be glorified. For starters, he is holy, honourable, righteous, resplendent, majestic, magnificent, mighty, strong, powerful, faithful, gracious, merciful, loving, kind, compassionate, omniscient and incomparable. But he is many other things as well.

Many of the psalms are unrestrained in their praise, adoration and exaltation of God's glory. Psalm 111:2-3, for example, says, "Great are the works of the LORD; they are pondered by all who delight in them. Glorious and majestic are his deeds, and his righteousness endures forever." It's as if, no matter how much we glorify his words, works and ways, he is always worthy of more.

We see a good example of this in Luke 1:26-38. The context here is that, having had an angelic visitation in which she's been told she will conceive by the Holy Spirit and give birth to Jesus, Mary has now discovered that her cousin, Elizabeth, is also pregnant – with John the Baptist.

Elizabeth and her husband Zechariah had been barren for years, in a culture where this would have been a deep source of shame. Now pregnant, God has totally turned around their tough time – and, in response, Mary erupts with joy, giving him all the glory in a beautiful song of praise, known as "the Magnificat" (Luke 1:46-55). "My soul glorifies the Lord," she sings, "and my spirit rejoices in God my Saviour."

Mary's Magnificat gives us so many reasons to glorify God. For instance, she rejoices: "For the Mighty One has done great things for me – holy is his name." In doing so, she reminds us of God's "might", referring to his power and strength to do anything, and his "holiness", signifying that he is sacred and set apart. Later, she sings, "His mercy extends to those who fear him, from generation to generation," reminding us of God's leniency with our sin.

The whole Magnificat resounds with Mary glorifying God, and her song can be ours too, for God is still mighty, holy, merciful and worthy of glory.

In "Building on God's Grace", Chapter 7 of *Light Through the Cracks*, we read the story of St Thomas' Church.

Early on in the story, following the threat of closure, God is gracious in providing the congregation with a supportive local vicar who speaks to the bishop on their behalf to grant them a reprieve.

God continues to be gracious when the bishop subsequently appoints an unpaid vicar, Phil, to lead St Thomas'. Over the years that follow, Phil and his wife Marian faithfully lead, serve and pray for the people in their congregation and community – and St Thomas' starts to grow.

Later, as Phil heads towards retirement, God is once again gracious to St Thomas'. Not only does he lead the right man to be their new vicar, but he also miraculously provides funds to pay for his salary.

Throughout the whole story, God keeps being gracious to St Thomas'. It's his grace that gets glorified.

***Pause:***

- Which of God's many attributes do you find it easiest to glorify, and why?

- **Secondly, we need to glorify God – because he made us for his glory**

By virtue of who he is, as ruler over all the earth, God made us for his glory. Isaiah 43:7 speaks of "everyone who is called by my name, whom I created for my glory, whom I formed and made."

This means our duty and delight is to glorify him at all times and in all circumstances: "So whether you eat or drink or whatever you do, do it all for the glory of God."[87] Indeed, "every nation, tribe, language and people" is expected to "fear God and give him glory."[88]

Because God made us for his glory, and he is the only one we are to glorify, he refuses to share his glory with anyone else.

87. 1 Corinthians 10:31
88. Revelation 14:6-7

"I am the LORD; that is my name!" he declares in Isaiah 42:8. "I will not yield my glory to another or my praise to idols." This means there are serious repercussions if we glorify anyone or anything else.

The demise of King Herod gives us an example of the severe judgement that God inflicts upon those who seize his glory for themselves. In Acts 12:21-23 we read how Herod put on his royal robes, sat on his throne and gave a speech to his people, as a result of which they glorify him, shouting, "This is the voice of a god, not of a man." Herod, however, does not rebuke them. Rather, he basks in their adulation, usurping the glory due only to God. As a consequence, he dies a gruesome death. "Immediately," we are told, "because Herod did not give praise to God, an angel of the Lord struck him down, and he was eaten by worms and died."

In tough times, it can be easy to inadvertently glorify medical professionals or others who help us, but what happened to Herod needs to stand as a lesson for us all.

In "Nothing Can Separate Us", Chapter 8 of *Light Through the Cracks*, we read the story of Jed, a boy who has a tragic hammock accident.

Throughout his story, his parents never fail to glorify God, particularly for his loving-kindness. No matter whether things are deteriorating or improving, they keep thanking God for his love for Jed, and for being in control.

Jed's parents know that God is at work through the medical professionals. So, when the neurologist alludes to the possibility that there might be a "higher power" at work on Jed's behalf, his parents agree. They know it is God alone who deserves all the glory.

***Pause:***

- What are your thoughts and feelings about God having made you for his glory?
- What could you do to remind yourself not to glorify other people in place of God?

- **Thirdly, we need to glorify God – because we need to seek his face before his hand**

When we are in a tough time it can be all too easy to focus on the miracle we want God to give us, but this isn't how he works. He doesn't want us to *seek first his hand.* He doesn't want us to seek first what he can give us, or do for us. He doesn't want us to seek first his help or assistance, his healing or comfort, his provision or protection.

Rather, he wants us to *seek first his face*. He wants us to seek first to know him, to love him, to adore him. He wants us to seek first to be in relationship with him – close friends, rather than casual acquaintances. He wants us to be in his presence, simply spending time with him, feeling safe, secure and held because we are with him.

It's a challenge that can be found throughout the Bible, and it's succinctly set out in 1 Chronicles 16:11, "Look to the LORD and his strength; seek his face always." Of equal challenge is our response – with God's desire being for us to echo the cry of Psalm 27:8, "My heart says of you, 'Seek his face!' Your face, LORD, I will seek."

God wants us to *know* him, not just know *about* him. He wants our focus to be more on who he is than on what he can do for us. He wants us to *seek first his face.*

In "Holding Onto a Prophetic Promise", Chapter 9 of *Light Through the Cracks*, we read the story of Henrik and Inger.

In the long and arduous months following Henrik's diagnosis of blood cancer, his wife Inger keeps seeking God's face. She knows that, whether or not they receive a miracle, God has given them a prophetic promise – and he is to be glorified while they wait for its fulfilment.

Henrik, too, knows that he is a beloved child of God. So, by focusing on this more than the miracle he longs for, he keeps giving God the glory.

***Pause:***

- Have you ever been tempted to seek God's hand, rather than his face? How could you turn this around if it happens again?

## WHAT: What is the biblical basis for glorifying God?

In John 11:1-44 we find an example of this principle being outworked in the story of Jesus with Mary, Martha and Lazarus.

In this story, life turns tough for these siblings. When Lazarus becomes ill, his sisters send for Jesus, but Jesus takes his time in coming. While they wait, Mary and Martha must make a life-changing choice. Will they glorify God, no matter what? Even if Lazarus dies, will they still give God the glory? The sisters make the choice to glorify God – and we can learn from their example.

It's a story that gives us four *keys* that we can use to *unlock* this principle.

- **KEY 1: Glorify God when he feels far away (John 11:1-4)**

  Now a man named Lazarus was ill. He was from Bethany, the village of Mary and her sister Martha. (This Mary, whose brother Lazarus now lay ill, was the same one who poured perfume on the Lord and wiped his feet with her hair.) So the sisters sent word to Jesus, "Lord, the one you love is sick."

  When he heard this, Jesus said, "This illness will not end in death. No, it is for God's glory so that God's Son may be glorified through it."

This story starts with Jesus having had to escape Jerusalem because the Jewish teachers of the Law have been threatening to stone him. He has headed twenty miles to the east, where he can be found on the banks of the River Jordan.[89]

It's here that a messenger comes to Jesus with a message from Mary and Martha to say that Lazarus, their brother and his beloved friend, is sick. We aren't told what condition he's got, but we can assume it's serious and life-threatening because the implication is that they would like Jesus to come straightaway. As some of his closest friends and supporters of his ministry,[90] it's not an unreasonable request. They know he has miraculous healing powers of the sort that could save their brother.

The siblings live in Bethany, less than two miles from Jerusalem,[91] so the messenger would have been walking for at least a day to reach Jesus. He would have been determined to cover the distance in as short a time as possible because of the urgency of the situation.

Yet Jesus' response seems strange. "This sickness will not end in death," he says, "No, it is for God's glory so that God's Son may be glorified through it."

What does he mean?

In a later verse we learn that Jesus waits two full days before travelling to Bethany, which takes at least a day to get to. We also learn that Jesus eventually arrives four days after Lazarus has died.[92] The reason this matters is that, by the time the messenger reaches Jesus, it's likely that Lazarus is already

89. See John 10:40
90. See Luke 10:38-42
91. John 11:18
92. John 11:6

dead. In fact, he probably died not long after the messenger was dispatched.

Yet here is Jesus sending him back with a message for Mary and Martha to say, "This sickness will not end in death." It's not exactly the comfort that the sisters are seeking – and it must have been so confusing to receive.

The fact is, Jesus knows that Lazarus has already died. Even as the messenger turns around and heads back to Bethany, Jesus knows that the sisters will have already buried their brother by the time the messenger reaches them. Nonetheless, he wants them to give God the glory.

***Pause:***

Maybe, like Mary, Martha and Lazarus, you are facing a tough time and Jesus feels far away. Maybe you have tried reaching out to him in prayer, but he just feels distant.

Maybe, across the distance, you have sensed Jesus speaking to you, but what he's saying just doesn't make sense.

If this is you, take a moment to give these feelings to God. Ask him to help you glorify him, even though he feels far away, and even though what he's saying seems to be confusing.

If we want to glorify God in our tough times no matter what, we need to give him the glory when he feels far away.

**KEY 2: Glorify God when he decides to delay (John 11:5-16)**

> Now Jesus loved Martha and her sister and Lazarus. So when he heard that Lazarus was ill, he stayed where he was two more days, and then he said to his disciples, "Let us go back to Judea."
>
> "But Rabbi," they said, "a short while ago the Jews there tried to stone you, and yet you are going back?"
>
> Jesus answered, "Are there not twelve hours of daylight? Anyone who walks in the daytime will not stumble, for they see by this world's light. It is when a person walks at night that they stumble, for they have no light."
>
> After he had said this, he went on to tell them, "Our friend Lazarus has fallen asleep; but I am going there to wake him up."
>
> His disciples replied, "Lord, if he sleeps, he will get better." Jesus had been speaking of his death, but his disciples thought he meant natural sleep.
>
> So then he told them plainly, "Lazarus is dead, and for your sake I am glad I was not there, so that you may believe. But let us go to him."
>
> Then Thomas (also known as Didymus) said to the rest of the disciples, "Let us also go, that we may die with him."

Given Jesus' love for these three siblings, and given he knows that Lazarus is already dead and buried, his decision to delay two days must have been baffling. Why did he not go straightaway to be with his grieving friends in their distress? His lack of haste must have looked cold and unfeeling – but he knows what he's doing, as we discover later.

The disciples assume it's because he doesn't want to be anywhere near Jerusalem, given the whole reason he's come to the River Jordan is to escape the Jews who were threatening to stone him, and they are frightened about the prospect of a return to Judea. But Jesus is quick to reassure them that he can safely return to Judea without fear, despite the threat of danger; that "twelve hours" gives enough time for what must be done, but no time to waste. Then, using a metaphor, he explains how he can clearly see the way because he's walking in the light of God's guidance, whereas he would be stumbling in the dark if he were not.

Jesus then refers to Lazarus' death as "sleep", a euphemism for death, commonly used in the culture at that time. But the disciples misunderstand, so he has to spell it out for them. "Lazarus is dead," he tells them plainly, and then, "I am glad I was not there, so that you may believe."

It feels perplexing for Jesus to express gladness in this context – and it's definitely not that he's happy or joyful about his friends' grief. It's more that he knows God's mighty resurrection power is about to be activated through him; that they are about to witness the most incredible miracle; that they will realise he is God's Son; and that this momentary pause in the timeline is going to lead to an amazing display of God's glory.

It also means Jesus' delay is deliberate. The timing of his arrival will be at precisely the right moment, and everyone else will have to trust him and stop leaning on their own understanding.[93]

Thomas understands this. He clearly thinks that journeying into Judea could potentially be a suicide mission, but he is willing to follow Jesus regardless. "Let us also go," he says, "that we may die with him."

***Pause:***

Maybe, like Mary and Martha, you are facing a tough time in which God seems to be inexplicably delayed in responding to your need. Maybe you have been praying for ages for a turnaround, and it feels as though God hasn't heard you, or has maybe abandoned you.

If this is you, give thanks to God that delays don't mean denial. Thank him for his timing, which is always perfect. Thank him for his purposes, which will always be worked out for your good and his glory.[94]

Maybe, like the disciples, you are facing a situation that could potentially be dangerous, and you need Jesus' reassurance that you will be safe with him, so you don't need to fear.

If this is you, confess and repent of any ways in which you have been leaning on your own understanding. Receive his forgiveness. Then ask him for fresh faith to trust him.

93. Proverbs 3:5-6
94. See Romans 8:28

If we want to glorify God in our tough times no matter what, we need to give him the glory when he feels far away, but also when he decides to delay.

- **KEY 3: Glorify God when he leaves it too late (John 11:17-32)**

  On his arrival, Jesus found that Lazarus had already been in the tomb for four days. Now Bethany was less than two miles from Jerusalem, and many Jews had come to Martha and Mary to comfort them in the loss of their brother. When Martha heard that Jesus was coming, she went out to meet him, but Mary stayed at home.

  "Lord," Martha said to Jesus, "if you had been here, my brother would not have died. But I know that even now God will give you whatever you ask."

  Jesus said to her, "Your brother will rise again."

  Martha answered, "I know he will rise again in the resurrection at the last day."

  Jesus said to her, "I am the resurrection and the life. The one who believes in me will live, even though they die; and whoever lives by believing in me will never die. Do you believe this?"

  "Yes, Lord," she replied, "I believe that you are the Messiah, the Son of God, who is to come into the world."

> After she had said this, she went back and called her sister Mary aside. "The Teacher is here," she said, "and is asking for you." When Mary heard this, she got up quickly and went to him. Now Jesus had not yet entered the village, but was still at the place where Martha had met him. When the Jews who had been with Mary in the house, comforting her, noticed how quickly she got up and went out, they followed her, supposing she was going to the tomb to mourn there.
>
> When Mary reached the place where Jesus was and saw him, she fell at his feet and said, "Lord, if you had been here, my brother would not have died."

When Jesus arrives in Bethany, he finds a desperate situation.

Jewish cultural belief at the time was that a dead person's spirit would linger near the body for *three* days after death, hoping to return to life. Beyond that timeframe, all hope would vanish and the body would begin to decompose. Thus, by the time Jesus gets there, at the end of the *fourth* day, Lazarus is conclusively dead.

He has also missed out on the initial phase of mourning, as many in the community have already paid their respects and come to console the sisters in their loss. This is because the Jewish custom, at that time, would have been for friends and neighbours to visit and comfort the family in the days immediately following the death.

Before he reaches the house, Martha comes out to meet him and, as she greets him, her grief is gut-wrenchingly raw. "Lord, if you had been here, my brother would not have died." Her words are laden with pain and blame, the implication clear. Jesus could have saved Lazarus' life. He could have saved her from this unbearable heartache and anguish. But he left it too late. He didn't come when they asked.

Even as Jesus assures her that her brother will rise again, she fails to understand that he has the power to raise Lazarus immediately and thinks he is referring solely to a future resurrection. So, to make it really clear, Jesus declares, "I am the resurrection and the life."

It is a profound and powerful pronouncement of his divine nature. Not only is he the source of both resurrection and life, he *is* life itself, so death has no hold on him.

Martha's response is incredible. "Yes, Lord," she states, "I believe that you are the Messiah." Not only is she publicly acknowledging Jesus' identity, but she is also affirming her trust in him. She is giving him glory through this powerful statement of faith – not knowing, at this stage, what the eventual outcome is going to be.

After such a transformative conversation, Martha doesn't want to keep things to herself. So she seeks out her sister with a sense of anticipation.

Mary's response is immediate. Jesus is asking for her and she needs to go to him urgently. It doesn't matter that some of the other mourners follow her; they need consoling as much as she does. "Lord, if you had been here," she says, falling at his feet, "my brother would not have died." Even though she doesn't understand why he left it too late, with words that are layered with grief and anguish, she still honours Jesus as "Lord". She still gives him glory.

***Pause:***

Maybe, like Mary and Martha, God has taken too long to come through for you in your tough time. Maybe it feels like he has left it too late, and things have gone from bad to worse. Maybe you are subtly blaming him for your pain.

If this is you, take a moment now to give God your thoughts and feelings. Confess and repent, if necessary, for any blame that you've laid at his feet. Then ask Jesus to show you how God can be glorified through his lateness.

If we want to glorify God in our tough times no matter what, we need to give him the glory when he feels far away, when he decides to delay and when he leaves it too late.

- **KEY 4: Glorify God when his power is displayed (John 11:33-44)**

  When Jesus saw her weeping, and the Jews who had come along with her also weeping, he was deeply moved in spirit and troubled. "Where have you laid him?" he asked.

  "Come and see, Lord," they replied.

  Jesus wept.

  Then the Jews said, "See how he loved him!"

> But some of them said, "Could not he who opened the eyes of the blind man have kept this man from dying?"
>
> Jesus, once more deeply moved, came to the tomb. It was a cave with a stone laid across the entrance. "Take away the stone," he said.
>
> "But, Lord," said Martha, the sister of the dead man, "by this time there is a bad odour, for he has been there four days."
>
> Then Jesus said, "Did I not tell you that if you believe, you will see the glory of God?"
>
> So they took away the stone. Then Jesus looked up and said, "Father, I thank you that you have heard me. I knew that you always hear me, but I said this for the benefit of the people standing here, that they may believe that you sent me."
>
> When he had said this, Jesus called in a loud voice, "Lazarus, come out!" The dead man came out, his hands and feet wrapped with strips of linen, and a cloth around his face.
>
> Jesus said to them, "Take off the grave clothes and let him go."

As Jesus witnesses this scene of mourning and grief, as he absorbs the loss and sorrow that is permeating the atmosphere, and as he sees Mary and the mourners weeping, he is deeply moved and troubled. Tears prick the backs of his eyes. His throat wells up. His chest heaves. He can't hold back the sobs. Jesus weeps.

His grief is visceral. His sense of loss is raw, real and relatable. It is also shared. He weeps with those who are weeping, cries with those who are crying, mourns with those who are mourning. He is right there with them, in the midst of their sorrow. He sees. He feels. He understands.

Picture the scene, tense with anticipation, as Jesus stands outside the tomb and orders the stone be taken away from the entrance. With a simple command, he reveals the importance of both faith and obedience in miracles. He reveals the need to hear what he's saying, trust his word, and act on it – even though it makes no sense. And he reveals the need to remove all obstacles that could stop God from getting the glory.

Ever pragmatic, Martha objects, knowing the body will have begun to decompose by now. It's a valid concern, and she no doubt voices what other onlookers are thinking. But Jesus reminds her that she needs to believe; that what is about to happen is going to glorify God.

So, the stone is moved out of the way, and Jesus then prays. He expresses gratitude to God, making it clear that what's about to happen is to be for his glory.

There is a collective intake of breath, everyone waiting and watching, as Jesus calls out in a loud voice, "Lazarus, come out!" And what happens next is extraordinary, as Lazarus emerges from the tomb, still wrapped in burial cloths, to everyone's utter astonishment.

It is a miraculous display of Jesus' power and authority over death, proving that he is, as he said to Martha, the resurrection and the life.

Amazement and joy replace mourning and grief, as the sisters and their friends help Lazarus remove his grave clothes, and give God all the glory.

***Pause:***

Maybe, like Mary, Martha and the other mourners, you simply need to know that Jesus weeps with you in your tough time. He sees your tears. He feels your pain. He grieves alongside you.

If this is you, take a moment to weep in God's presence. Allow him to love, hug and hold you. Let him show you how much he understands what you are going through.

Maybe, like Lazarus, you are in need of some sort of resurrection in your tough time. Maybe you need the stone or other obstacle to be moved out of the way,[95] through faith and obedience, before that can happen. Or maybe the resurrection has happened, but you are still wrapped in grave clothes and you need the things encasing you to be removed.

If this is you, take a moment to bring the thing that has "died" before God and ask him to "resurrect" it. If he shows you that there is an obstacle in the way, let him move it aside. And if you have already received resurrection, let him remove anything that is encasing you, so that you can experience full freedom and release.

95. For more on this, please see Chapter 3, "Let Go".

If we want to glorify God in our tough times no matter what, we need to give him the glory when he feels far away, when he decides to delay, when he leaves it too late, and when his power is displayed.

When Mary and Martha send for Jesus, they expect him to come straightaway, but he chooses to delay. When Lazarus dies, the sisters have to bury their brother, knowing that Jesus could have healed him. But even if this remains the ultimate outcome, they are still prepared to glorify God. When they later receive a miracle, God gets even more glory.

## HOW: How can we glorify God, whatever the outcome, in practice?

The good news is that glorifying God is a skill that can be learnt.

In 1 Chronicles 16, David appoints some of the Levites to minister, extol, thank and praise the LORD,[96] giving us a model for how to glorify God.

"Give praise to the LORD, proclaim his name; make known among the nations what he has done," he instructs in verses 8-11. "Sing to him, sing praise to him; tell of all his wonderful acts. Glory in his holy name; let the hearts of those who seek the LORD rejoice. Look to the LORD and his strength; seek his face always."

96. 1 Chronicles 16:4

What a wonderful set of verbs these verses contain, any of which we can emulate.

Also, in case we need any reasons for giving God glory, David gives us plenty in verses 25-29: "For great is the LORD and most worthy of praise; he is to be feared above all gods . . . Splendour and majesty are before him; strength and joy are in his dwelling-place . . . Ascribe to the LORD the glory due his name; bring an offering and come before him. Worship the LORD in the splendour of his holiness." It means we are without excuse!

So, what can we do, practically, to glorify God, whatever the outcome?

- **Glorify God – by praising and thanking him**

When you praise God, you are *joyfully recounting* all he has done. When you thank him, you are *expressing gratitude and appreciation* for all he has done. As a result, the two are often closely connected. Hence, for example, the call of Psalm 100:4 to "Enter his gates with thanksgiving and his courts with praise; give thanks to him and praise his name."

"Praise the Lord" is a constant refrain in the Bible, especially in the Psalms, where it is often portrayed as energetic, lively, jubilant and uninhibited. You can praise God with singing,[97] shouting,[98] a joyful noise,[99] lifting hands,[100] dancing[101] and musical instruments.[102] It is such an important mandate that

97. Psalm 9:11, Isaiah 12:5
98. Psalm 98:4
99. Psalm 33:1
100. Psalm 63:4
101. Psalm 150:4
102. Psalm 108:2, Psalm 150:3-5, 1 Chronicles 13:8

Jesus says in Luke 19:40 that even "the stones will cry out" if people won't praise God!

Thankfulness is also a call that weaves throughout the Bible. "Rejoice always, pray continually," says 1 Thessalonians 5:16-18, "give thanks in *all* circumstances; for this is God's will for you in Christ Jesus" (italics mine). In writing this, Paul is assuming that thankfulness is such a normal way of life for followers of Jesus, that it will naturally overflow in *all* circumstances, including tough times.

In Psalm 28:6-7 David gives praise and thanks to God *in the midst of* a tough time: "Praise be to the LORD, for he has heard my cry for mercy. The LORD is my strength and my shield; my heart trusts in him, and he helps me. My heart leaps for joy, and with my song I praise him." And in Psalm 30:1-12, he gives thanks and praise to God, *following* a tough time: "I will exalt you, LORD, for you lifted me out of the depths," he says. "You turned my wailing into dancing; you removed my sackcloth and clothed me with joy, that my heart may sing to you and not be silent. LORD my God, I will praise you for ever."

Peter, too, speaks of being thankful for "grief in all kinds of trials,"[103] saying that, because of them, your faith may be proved genuine and "may result in praise, glory and honour when Jesus Christ is revealed".

The more you learn to praise and thank God, the more you will remember all that he has done, is doing, and will do for you. This, in turn, will remind you that he is in control,

103. 1 Peter 1:6-7

which will enable you to glorify him no matter what is happening in your tough time.

- **Glorify God – by worshipping him**

Whereas praise and thanksgiving focus on what God has done, worship focuses on who he is. Many people associate "worship" with singing songs in church. However, genuine worship is not an activity reserved for Sunday services; it's a lifestyle reserved for God alone. It's why Jesus says in Luke 4:8, "Worship the Lord your God and serve him only."[104]

God is seeking people who will worship him "in [Holy] Spirit and in truth".[105] This means that true worship starts with the attitude and posture of your heart. It requires you to humble yourself before God, relinquishing every part of your life to his control, and then adoring and glorifying him for who he is. To demonstrate this sort of surrender, you might want to consider coupling your worship with actions that demonstrate humility and contrition, such as bowing down[106] or falling on your knees[107] before God.

True worship is costly, which Paul acknowledges in Romans 12:1. "I urge you, brothers and sisters," he says, "in view of God's mercy, to offer your bodies as a living sacrifice, holy and pleasing to God – this is your true and proper worship." The implication is clear: your worship must be motivated by a profound recognition of all God has given you, which has been unmerited and undeserved, and it must involve a

104. Jesus, here, is quoting Deuteronomy 6:13
105. John 4:23
106. Psalm 95:6, 2 Chronicles 29:28
107. Revelation 19:10

sacrificial offering of the whole of your life. This combination is "your true and proper worship".

In Romans 12:2 Paul explains what this looks like in practice: "Do not conform to the pattern of this world," he says, "but be transformed by the renewing of your mind. Then you will be able to test and approve what God's will is – his good, pleasing and perfect will." In this sense, "the world" refers to "the lust of the flesh, the lust of the eyes, and the pride of life",[108] so the call is to resist these things; to sacrifice them. Then you will be transformed, your mind will be renewed, and your worship will be "holy and pleasing to God".

This is why the Bible calls you to "worship the LORD in the splendour of his holiness".[109] It is because his holiness detests your sin. So you have got to get the posture of your heart right before him, through confession, repentance and surrender, so that you can come into his presence and worship him, humble and contrite. That's the stance from which you will learn how to glorify him, whatever the outcome of your tough time.

- **Glorify God – by honouring him**

When you honour God, you glorify him, and one way to honour him is to live your life with integrity. The Hebrew concept of "integrity" comes from a word meaning "being without blemish, completeness, perfection, sincerity, soundness and uprightness". It is closely connected with holiness, which involves being "set apart" from sin and evil[110] in order to be consecrated to God.

108. 1 John 2:15-17
109. Psalm 96:9
110. 1 John 1:5-7

God calls you to be holy, just as he is.[111] However, this is impossible without salvation through what Jesus' accomplished on the cross by his death and resurrection, and without the indwelling empowering of the Holy Spirit. So, if you have accepted Jesus as your Saviour, and if you are regularly being filled with the Holy Spirit, it is from this position that you will be able to live a life that is honouring to God – through things like sexual purity,[112] obedience to God,[113] freedom from sin,[114] being accountable to other believers,[115] and serving.[116]

What's important to remember is that the purpose of living your life with integrity and holiness is to honour and glorify God. As Matthew 5:16 says, "Let your light shine before others, that they may see your good deeds and glorify your Father in heaven."

The way that you handle your tough time can speak volumes to those around you!

***Pause:***

- What has God done for you, for which you can praise and thank him?
- Which of God's attributes most prompts you to worship him for who he is?
- How are you honouring God in your lifestyle, and what could you do differently to get better at it?

111. 1 Peter 1:16, Leviticus 19:2
112. 1 Thessalonians 4:3-8
113. 1 Peter 1:14-16
114. Romans 6:6
115. Hebrews 10:24-25
116. 1 Peter 4:10

## Digging Deeper

Now could be a good time to practise glorifying God.

**Exercise**

- Invite the Holy Spirit to come and be present.
- Slowly read Psalm 103. Pause whenever you notice an aspect of God's character being described, and make a note of it in your notebook or journal (or on your digital device).
- Look at your notes and ask yourself: which of God's characteristics most resonates with you, and why? Give your response to this to God in prayer.
- Take time to give thanks to God for who he is, using sung worship. Choose one or more of the songs listed below to get you started.

If you are doing this exercise with others, you could read the whole of Psalm 103 together, and then verbally share the characteristics of God that it mentions. You could also discuss which ones most resonate with you, and why.

## Worship Songs

- "Glorify Thy Name" by Donna Adkins.
- "Tell Out My Soul" by Timothy Dudley-Smith.
- "Blessed Be Your Name" by Matt and Beth Redman.
- "Worthy" (Elevation Worship) by Chris Brown, Mack Brock and Steven Furtick.

## Further Reading

- *Worshipping God: Devoting Our Lives to His Glory* by R.T. Kendall.

### Additional questions for small groups

- How good are we, between us, at giving glory to God?
- What could we do to get better at glorifying God, especially if one or more of us are going through a tough time?

CHAPTER 6

# Testify

## When life turns tough, will you share the story of what God has done?

*"Come and hear, all you who fear God;*
*let me tell you what he has done for me."*
(Psalm 66:16)

### Introduction

When life turns tough, we face a choice.

Will we testify to what God has done for us during our tough times? Will we make sure our friends, family, church community and others all hear about it? Or will we keep it to ourselves? Where our story contains difficult or challenging aspects, will we still share them? Or will we sugar-coat, sanitise or remove them?

God's desire is for us to share our testimony stories, especially during and after tough times, but we have to be intentional about it. Testifying starts when we choose to recognise what God has done and then tell other people about it.

## WHERE: Where did the idea of testifying to what God has done for us originate?

To "testify" describes the act of bearing witness to, or giving evidence about, the truth of something. It's a word that is often used in a courtroom setting.

In the Bible, the word "testimony" comes from a Hebrew word that means "to testify or bear witness". It refers to the act of proclaiming our first-hand accounts of who God is and what he has done for us, based on our personal experiences. So it's in this sense that I am using the word "testify" in this chapter.

The reason for this is that, at its core, *Light Through the Cracks* is a collection of stories that testify to what God has done in the midst of tough times. If the people involved had not shared their testimonies, the book would not exist! It's a central theme.[117]

In addition to sharing their stories in *Light Through the Cracks*, there are a variety of other ways in which the people involved have testified to what God has done for them in their tough times. From featuring in national television programmes to appearing on local radio shows; from sharing short film clips on social media to writing articles for parish magazines; from

117. It also means there are a small number of spoilers in this chapter, which cannot be avoided.

being interviewed in the context of Sunday morning church services to standing on platforms at conferences; from chatting in informal conversations around the dinner table to telling complete strangers while out and about – the variety of ways to testify are as varied as the stories themselves.

What matters is that the people involved are able to recognise what God has done for them in their tough times, and are then prepared to share their stories with as many people as possible.

In "All It Takes Is One Split Second", Chapter 4 of *Light Through the Cracks*, we read the story of Adrian and Ruth, and their horrific head-on car crash.

Adrian's injuries are so severe that we are told, on more than one occasion, he might die. But God gives us Psalm 118:17 to hold onto: "[He] will not die but live, and will proclaim what the LORD has done." So our prayers trust God, not just for his life, but also his testimony.

Many months later, Adrian and Ruth testify to "what the LORD has done" at church, on local radio and in various other settings.

***Pause:***

- Can you recall a testimony story that has impacted your life? How did the people involved testify to what God has done for them? Why do you think the story has stayed with you?

## WHY: Why do we need to testify to what God has done for us?

I would like to suggest there are four reasons why we need to testify to what God has done for us.

- **Firstly, we need to testify to what God has done – because every testimony story is unique**

It's been said that everyone has a story inside them. If we've been through a tough time in which God showed up for us, we've been given a unique testimony story!

We might be tempted to think that our story isn't exciting enough, doesn't contain sufficient drama, and will be of no interest to anyone beyond our immediate family and closest friends, but this simply isn't true! If God has chosen to work in our lives during tough times, he will have done so for a reason. Whether or not we are able to identify the reason, our job is simply to testify about it.

It doesn't matter whether God has broken into our tough time through supernatural miracles or the seemingly mundane. It doesn't matter whether our story involves lots of little God moments or a single spectacular mind-blowing event. What matters is that we share our first-hand account of where we have found God's "*light through the cracks*".

If we can testify to how God has worked in our life, broken into our tough time, helped us find faith in Jesus, blessed and encouraged us, healed and delivered us, provided for our needs or protected us from danger, nobody can argue with our experience, because our stories are uniquely personal to us.

Nobody else has the same story – or the same perspective on a shared story – as us. It's down to us to ensure that we testify to it, so that people hear it.

In "X-rays Never Lie", Chapter 2 of *Light Through the Cracks*, we read the story of Keith, who has an unexpected stroke and also finds a tumour on his adrenal gland.

He knows of nobody else with the same combination of ailments as he has had, but he knows there will be those who can relate. So, at the end of his story, we see him standing in front of a packed church, testifying to God's goodness.

***Pause:***

- What testimony stories do you have of God breaking into a tough time in your life? What aspects of these testimonies make them uniquely yours?

- **Secondly, we need to testify to what God has done – because God instructs us to remember**

In Deuteronomy 4:9 God says to his people, "Do not forget the things your eyes have seen or let them fade from your heart as long as you live," with instructions to pass these eye-witness stories onto their children and grandchildren. It's one of the reasons why the Jewish people, during the Passover and their other annual feasts, place so much importance on remembering the details of God's miracles. It's a tradition that has been handed down through hundreds of generations.

The same goes for us! We need to remember what God has done and testify to it, something I referenced in my introduction to *Light Through the Cracks*:

> In the Bible, the word "remember" occurs over 230 times, and frequently in conjunction with a call to celebrate. It is clear that God wants people to remember and celebrate what he has done . . .
>
> When God performed miracles in the Bible, the people built piles of stones and gave the places new names. Each time the people passed by, as they wandered through the land, they would remember and celebrate what God had done – with each generation passing the stories down to the next, until they were written down.
>
> In the 21st century, we need a modern-day equivalent of piles of stones and new place names. We need to share and record the stories. We need to remember and celebrate, rather than forget.

In Joshua chapters 3 and 4 we are given a good example. It's a story in which God miraculously parts the waters of the River Jordan while it is in flood, which enables his people to walk across on dry ground and enter the promised land. As they camp overnight at Gilgal, Joshua erects a memorial comprising twelve stones taken from the river, one each for the twelve tribes of Israel.

Then he says to the people: "In the future when your descendants ask their parents, 'What do these stones mean?' tell them, 'Israel crossed the Jordan on dry ground.' For the LORD your God dried up the Jordan before you until you had crossed over." And then he explains why this needs to be remembered. God, he says, "did this so that all the peoples of the earth might know that the hand of the LORD is powerful and so that you might always fear the LORD your God".[118]

We, too, need to remember and testify to the times when we have witnessed the hand of God in our lives.

In "Synchronisation Is His Watchword", Chapter 1 of *Light Through the Cracks*, I tell the story of the car accident that I was in, with my brother, while we were on holiday in the USA.

After I return to the UK, encased in a back brace, many friends and family members urge me to write down all the details – just in case, one day, they may end up in a book! I do as suggested and note everything down in my journal.

Later, these notes and reflections enable me to remember the specifics of what happened, so that I can testify to what God has done in writing the opening chapter of *Light Through the Cracks*.

They also enable me to testify to the ways God helped us, whenever I am invited to speak about the car accident.

118. Joshua 4:20-24

***Pause:***

- What can you do to remind yourself of who God is and what he has done for you? If the instruction to "remember" is new to you, what could you do to aid your memory of God's involvement in your tough times?

- **Thirdly, we need to testify – because the word of our testimony is a weapon of spiritual warfare**

In Revelation 12:11 we read how Christian believers can overcome the Enemy through two weapons of spiritual warfare: "They triumphed over him by the blood of the Lamb and by the word of their testimony; they did not love their lives so much as to shrink from death."

The first weapon is "the blood of the Lamb", which is a reference to Jesus' sacrificial death on the cross when he defeated Satan once and for all.[119] But the second is "the word of [our] testimony". This means that, whenever we testify to what God has done or is doing in our lives, we can triumph over the Enemy! It's a powerful weapon for use in the spiritual battle.

An example of this can be found in 1 Samuel 17, where David is preparing to slay Goliath, the giant who is leading the enemy army against God's people. As David gets ready, King Saul expresses concern over David's suitability as a soldier.

119. See Chapter 4, "Solidify" for more on this.

Undeterred by Saul's assessment, David simply testifies to what God has done for him in the past, completely confident that God will do it again. "The Lord who rescued me from the paw of the lion and the paw of the bear will rescue me from the hand of this Philistine."[120]

The word of David's testimony plays a powerful part in securing his victory over Goliath, because it declares his utter reliance on God. And we can have the same assurance, as we face our own giants, but we have to make a decision. Will we confidently recall and declare God's good track record? Will we rely on him alone to defeat the Enemy?

Testifying to God's goodness, protection, power or any of his other attributes – preferably out loud – shifts things in the spiritual atmosphere. It reminds the Enemy of who God is. It reminds the Enemy that God can, and likely will, do it again. And it reminds the Enemy that he is a defeated foe; Jesus has triumphed.

> In "Power In the Name of Jesus", Chapter 3 of *Light Through the Cracks*, we read the story of Karen who is diagnosed with stomach cancer.
>
> With faith-filled insistence, she pronounces her belief that the cancer is not of God. Having seen miracles while living in Cape Town, she knows that Jesus can heal her. "He that is in us is greater than he that is in the world," she reminds her prayer supporters.

120. 1 Samuel 17:37

Significant spiritual warfare follows, resulting in God giving Karen an incredible testimony. "Jesus has saved my life," she tells everyone who will listen.

***Pause:***

- How could you use "the word of your testimony" to wage spiritual warfare over the aspects of your tough time, which are part of the spiritual battle?

- **Fourthly, we need to testify – because it is an effective tool for evangelism**

Sceptics may debate the validity of the Scriptures, or argue against the existence of God, but nobody can argue with an authentic personal testimony – and if it points people to Jesus, they might just decide to put their faith in him.

Stories are more persuasive than intellectual debates because they are based on first-hand experiences. They connect with the heart, not the head. They speak of relationship, not religion.

In John 4 we read about a Samaritan woman who comes across Jesus at a well. Her encounter with him has such a profound impact that, when she returns to her community, she testifies about it to everyone who will listen. "Then, leaving her water jar, the woman went back to the town and said to the people, 'Come, see a man who told me everything I've ever done. Could this be the Messiah?' They came out of the town and made their way towards him."[121] As a result,

121. John 4:28-30

"Many of the Samaritans from that town believed in [Jesus] because of the woman's testimony."[122]

Just like the Samaritan woman, when we have an encounter with Jesus we can invite people to meet him. We can share how God has broken into our tough times. We can open people's hearts to the possibility of a relationship with him.

Sometimes, it works the other way around. 1 Peter 3:15-16 encourages us to "always be prepared to give an answer to everyone who asks you to give the reason for the hope that you have. But do this with gentleness and respect, keeping a clear conscience". This means that we need to be ready to share our faith at any moment – and one of the best ways to do this is through testifying to what God has done in our lives.

Testimony stories are an effective tool for evangelism.

In "Release From a Prison of Darkness", Chapter 10 of *Light Through the Cracks*, we read the story of Anna, the talented teenage dancer who becomes unwell with ME.

Even at a young age, she doesn't hold back from talking about Jesus with anyone who will listen. But after God heals her, this becomes even more pronounced.

Having been so restricted by her illness, she radiates gratitude and joy, seizing every opportunity to testify to what God has done. As a result, many people find faith in Jesus.

122. John 4:39

***Pause:***

- In what ways could you testify to what God has done in your life with your friends and family who don't yet know Jesus?

**WHAT: What is the biblical basis for testifying to what God has done for us?**

In John 9:1-12 we find an example of this principle being outworked in the story of Jesus with a man born blind.

In this story, the blind man has a tough life, spending his days begging by the roadside, not far from the temple. When Jesus restores his sight, he has a choice to make. Will he keep his miraculous healing to himself? Or will he testify to what God has done for him?

He makes the choice to testify – and we can learn from his example.

It's a story that gives us three *keys* that we can use to *unlock* this principle: *confirmation, transformation* and *proclamation.*

- **KEY 1: Confirmation of the facts (John 9:1-5)**

  As he went along, he saw a man blind from birth. His disciples asked him, "Rabbi, who sinned, this man or his parents, that he was born blind?"

  "Neither this man nor his parents sinned," said Jesus, "but this happened so that the works of God might

> be displayed in him. As long as it is day, we must do the works of him who sent me. Night is coming, when no one can work. While I am in the world, I am the light of the world."

This story starts as Jesus is slipping away from the temple grounds in Jerusalem. He has only just narrowly escaped being stoned, following a heated discourse with the Jewish teachers of the Law in which he has claimed to be "I AM", the name God originally revealed to Moses.[123]

Now, as he walks along, accompanied by his disciples, he sees a blind man sitting at the side of the road – and he instantly knows he's been blind since birth. The blind man is oblivious. He's just doing what he does every day. But it's Jesus who notices him. It's Jesus who is being observant. It's Jesus who initiates their interaction that day.

Immediately, the disciples raise an age-old question, generated by so many people when they witness suffering in the world: "Rabbi, who sinned, this man or his parents, that he was born blind?" In other words: *why?* And because Jesus is with them, they direct their question at him, and he confirms the facts.

In that culture, it was commonly assumed that if a person was born with an affliction, it had been caused by sin. Either sin in the womb – or sin committed in a previous generation, which comes from the biblical concept of "generational iniquity", in which God warns that he is "a jealous God, punishing the children for the sins of the parents to the

123. Exodus 3:14

third and fourth generation of those who hate [him]".[124] The implication is that ungodly fathers raise rebellious children, who choose to repeat their sinful lifestyles, passing them on from generation to generation – unless and until there is repentance and the sin stops.

Jesus goes on to explain that the actual reason for the man's condition is "so that the works of God might be displayed in him".

He knows that God is about to do a miracle. He knows that God is about to do such a powerful work of healing in this man that he will, for the rest of his life, display God's glory – and God's light. Not only will he see natural daylight for the first time ever, having been in darkness for his entire life, but he will also see Jesus, "the light of the world".[125]

This man will, quite literally, be a living testimony to God's glory, light and power – and it's solely for this reason that he was born blind!

Jesus, through this explanation, is giving the blind man confirmation of the facts: yes, he was born blind; but no, it was not because of sin. Rather, it was so that he might display God's works.

***Pause:***

When we testify to what God has done in our tough times, our starting point is usually to give some context to our hearers through confirmation of the facts.

124. Exodus 20:5 and 34 :7, Numbers 14:18, Deuteronomy 5:9
125. John 8:12

What are the facts that give the context to your testimony story?

Maybe, like the blind man, you were doing what you always do, getting on with life, minding your own business – but then Jesus saw you, noticed you, initiated an interaction with you.

Maybe, like the blind man, you overheard Jesus saying how God wants to display his works in your life – and you were astounded.

Or maybe, like the disciples, you were wrestling with questions about why there is suffering in the world – only for Jesus to shatter your assumptions and set you straight.

Take a moment to reflect on the context for your tough time. Ask the Holy Spirit to help you remember all the facts and make a note of them. Include your thoughts and feelings about your situation as it was at the outset. Then give them to God in prayer.

If we want to testify to what God has done for us in our tough times, we need to start with confirmation of the facts.

- **KEY 2: Transformation of the tough time (John 9:6-7)**

  After saying this, he spat on the ground, made some mud with the saliva, and put it on the man's eyes.

> "Go," he told him, "wash in the Pool of Siloam" (this word means "Sent"). So the man went and washed, and came home seeing.

The blind man, sitting at the side of the road, must have felt such mixed emotions, overhearing the conversation that has just unfolded high above his head. What a relief to know that his blindness hasn't been caused by his or his parents' sin! But what on earth did Jesus mean, saying that God's works would be displayed in his life?

Before he can ask, he can hear the sound of someone spitting, followed by a pregnant pause. A few moments later, he can feel the touch of a mud-spattered hand on his eyes. Then he hears Jesus speaking.

Interestingly, this is one of only three instances in the Gospels in which Jesus uses his spittle in the process of healing.[126] At that time, contemporary culture considered saliva to have significant medicinal healing properties, making it a valid treatment for blindness. So, the blind man in this story would have naturally interpreted Jesus' spitting as a sign he would soon be cured.

What follows is the blind man's obedience to Jesus' instructions. "Go," he says, "wash in the pool of Siloam," and then John adds a note: "This word means 'Sent'." In other words, the blind man was *sent* to a pool called "*Sent*", by the one who God had *sent* into the world!

There was a practical reason for this, because the pool of Siloam was the only source of *fresh* water within the walls

126. The others are recorded in Mark 7:33 and Mark 8:23.

of ancient Jerusalem, as it was fed by the Gihon Spring, via a tunnel built by King Hezekiah, which cut through solid rock. The poor and the sick often came to bathe there, so the blind man, with his mud-covered eyes, wouldn't have been out of place, obeying Jesus' instruction to wash there.

Then he comes home seeing! What an incredible transformation! He sets off for the pool, blind, returning with his sight restored.

His spiritual eyes are also opened. "I believe," we hear him declaring later, in John 9:38, as he worships Jesus.

***Pause:***

When we testify to what God has done, at the heart of the story will be the transformation of our tough time, the pivot point when he broke in and things began to turn around.

When, in your testimony story, has transformation happened?

Maybe, like this blind man, you felt Jesus touching your life, or you heard him speaking personally to you, or both. Maybe Jesus asked you to do something specific and you obeyed, as a result of which you experienced a turnaround.

Take a moment to reflect on when, in your tough time, transformation has taken place. There might have been one main pivot point, or several small ones along the way. Note down all that you can recall. Then give thanks to God for the way he has turned things around for you.

If we want to testify to what God has done for us in our tough times, we need to start with confirmation of the facts, then describe the transformation that has taken place.

- **KEY 3: Proclamation of what God has done (John 9:8-12)**

  His neighbours and those who had formerly seen him begging asked, "Isn't this the same man who used to sit and beg?" Some claimed that he was.

  Others said, "No, he only looks like him."

  But he himself insisted, "I am the man."

  "How then were your eyes opened?" they asked.

  He replied, "The man they call Jesus made some mud and put it on my eyes. He told me to go to Siloam and wash. So I went and washed, and then I could see."

  "Where is this man?" they asked him.

  "I don't know," he said.

Don't you love the reaction of the now-formerly-blind man's friends and neighbours?

He has returned home, *his eyes now seeing*, yet they can't quite believe what *their eyes are seeing*! It simply makes no sense – and the irony is delightful!

While the formerly-blind man has brand-new eyesight and is able to see clearly, it's his friends and neighbours who are now "blind" and unable to see – and it causes a ruckus. Some of them claim that it has to be the same man they have walked past, daily, for decades. Others decide it can't be; it must just be his lookalike.

Into the fray the man himself speaks, insisting he is the one they are discussing; the one who used to be blind. "How then were your eyes opened?" the baffled onlookers ask, and the man responds with grace and clarity. "The man they call Jesus made some mud and put it on my eyes," he explains. "He told me to go to Siloam and wash. So I went and washed, and then I could see."

It is an exemplary way of testifying to how God has broken into his tough time. It's a proclamation that is bold, truthful and succinct. It's a proclamation of his first-hand account. It's also a proclamation that points people to Jesus.

"Where is this man?" the people ask him, and it doesn't matter that he doesn't know. What matters is that an interest in Jesus has been ignited, because this man told them his story.

***Pause:***

When we testify to what God has done in our tough times, what matters most is the proclamation of the story in ways that give God all the glory.[127]

In what ways have you proclaimed, or could you proclaim, your testimony story?

Maybe, like the formerly-blind man, you have friends and neighbours who have seen the transformation

127. See Chapter 5, "Glorify", for more on this.

in your life and are open to you telling them how it happened. Maybe, like him, you have a clear and simple testimony which could impact those who God has placed around you.

Now consider your own testimony story. In what ways could you be bold, truthful and succinct in proclaiming it? How could you point people to Jesus as you do so?

Take a moment to thank God for how he has broken into your tough time, and for the testimony story he has given you. Ask him for opportunities to proclaim it, and commit to seizing them when they arise.

If we want to testify to what God has done for us in our tough time, we need to start with confirmation of the facts, then describe the transformation that has taken place, before finishing with proclamation that gives God the glory.

When the blind man set out from home that day, he had no idea that Jesus would see him, stop for him and miraculously heal him. But it gave him a powerful first-hand account of how God broke into his tough time, to which he could repeatedly testify.

### HOW: How can we testify to what God has done for us in practice?

The good news is that testifying is a skill that can be learnt! Even the most reticent or reluctant person can share their testimony of what God has done.

"I did not come with eloquence or human wisdom as I proclaimed to you the testimony about God," Paul says in 1 Corinthians 2:1, making it clear that our testimonies need to be proclaimed, even if we feel foolish or inarticulate.

"For I resolved to know nothing while I was with you except Jesus Christ and him crucified," he continues in verse 2, reminding us to point people to Jesus through what we proclaim.

"I came to you in weakness with great fear and trembling," he adds in verse 3, encouraging all of us to push through our feelings of weakness and fear.

Then finally, "My message and my preaching were not with wise and persuasive words, but with a demonstration of the Spirit's power, so that your faith might not rest on human wisdom, but on God's power," he says in verses 4-5, inspiring us to let the Holy Spirit's power, rather than our words or wisdom, persuade people of the truth of our testimonies.

So, what can we do, practically, to learn to testify to what God has done for us?

- **Testify to what God has done – by believing your story needs telling**

Whether you are instinctively shy and diffident, or naturally bold and confident, your mindset will impact your ability to testify. So invite the Holy Spirit to renew your mind and transform your thinking[128] so that you're able to see your

128. Romans 12:2

story as God sees it – uniquely yours and one that the world needs to hear.

Remember that there will be people going through tough times, which are similar to yours, and God wants them to hear how he has helped you so that he can raise their faith to believe he can do the same for them.

- **Testify to what God has done – by working out what to say**

Every story, whether simple or complex, has a *beginning*, a *middle* and an *end* – and this includes testimony stories.

Paul gives us a good example. On at least three occasions[129] he testifies to how he was persecuting people who believed in Jesus (his *beginning*), until he had a powerful and personal encounter with Jesus on the road to Damascus (the *middle*), which turned his life around and led to God using him to spread the message of Jesus to non-Jewish people (the *end*).

With this in mind, commit to write out the content of your testimony by doing the exercise at the end of this chapter, and then to practise sharing it. Remember to include a way for your hearers to respond. In Paul's case, he always invited his hearers to find faith in Jesus for themselves, but you might want to offer a different response.

- **Testify to what God has done – by relying on the Holy Spirit**

Whenever you testify, remember that 1 John 5:6 says, "It is the Spirit who testifies, because the Spirit is truth." This

129. It is recorded three times, in Acts 9:1-9, Acts 22:3-21 and Acts 26:4-23

means you can ask God to fill you with his Holy Spirit and then rely on him to help you, trusting that he will equip and empower you with all that you need.

All the Holy Spirit needs is for you to testify to the straightforward truth of what God has done in your tough time, so that he can point people to Jesus. He will equip and empower you to be open and vulnerable, guarding what needs to be kept private, while honestly sharing what needs to be told.

- **Testify to what God has done – by making the most of every opportunity**

There are many ways of testifying to how God breaks into tough times – from one-on-one conversations with friends, to conference platforms in front of hundreds; from simple social media posts, to national newspaper articles; plus everything in between.

What matters is that you are making the most of every opportunity,[130] always ready to give an answer to anyone who asks,[131] and willing to testify to what God has done.

***Pause:***

- In what ways have you testified, or could you testify, and to whom, about how God has broken, or is breaking, into your tough time?
- What might hold you back from testifying, and how could you overcome these barriers?

130. Ephesians 5:16
131. 1 Peter 3:15

## Digging Deeper

Now could be a good time to practise testifying to what God has done in your tough time.

**Exercise**

- Invite the Holy Spirit to guide your thoughts and reveal his presence.
- Consider the tough time you are currently facing, or ask God to bring to mind a tough time you have faced in the past, showing you where he is or was present in it.
- Now take a clean sheet of paper in your notebook or journal (or on your digital device) and divide it into three sections, labelling them, one each: *Before*, *During* and *After*.
- Using the following suggestions, take time to work out the content for each part of your testimony by noting ideas in each of the three sections on your sheet of paper:

    *Before:* Set the scene for how your tough time started. State the facts, as clearly and concisely as possible. Use language that is relatable and free of religious jargon.

    *During:* Accurately describe the ways in which God has revealed himself throughout your tough time and what he has done for you. If it has happened gradually, refer to each stage of change; if sudden, refer to the pivot point, when everything turned around. Leave out confusing tangents and elaborate details. Make it easy to follow.

*After:* Testify to the difference in your life since God turned your tough time around, giving him the glory as you do so. Be authentic in sharing your thoughts and feelings. Include an invitation to your hearers to respond.

- Now take a moment to give your notes to God, asking him to give you opportunities to share your testimony. If any names come to mind, write them in your notebook or journal (or on your digital device) and commit to meet up with them or phone them, depending on how near they live. If helpful, ask someone you trust to hold you accountable for following through on this.
- End by giving thanks to God for the testimony he has given you.

Remember that when you testify to what God has done for you, the way you do it does not need to be perfect. What matters more is that you give it a go!

If you are doing this exercise with others, you could practise sharing your testimonies with each other. You could also hold each other accountable for sharing your testimonies with those in your lives who are not yet Christians, and give yourselves a deadline for everyone to feed back to the group about how it has gone.

## Worship Songs

- "Goodness of God" (Bethel Worship) by Ed Cash, Ben Fielding, Jason Ingram, Brian Johnson and Jenn Johnson.
- "My Testimony" (Elevation Worship) by Chris Brown, Steven Furtick, Brandon Lake and Tiffany Hudson.

## Further Reading

- *Remember* by Richard Gamble.

### Additional questions for small groups

- What can we do, practically, to share our testimonies together on a more regular basis? How might this encourage our faith in Jesus?
- What can we do to support each other to testify to the people in our lives who are not yet Christians? How could we hold each other accountable for this?

# Frequently Asked Questions

I hope you enjoyed reading *It's All About the Light* and that each of the biblical principles has challenged you to make life-changing choices, and deepened your understanding of the ways God has given us to find him in our tough times, whether that applies to your own situation or that of a loved one. I also hope you encountered Jesus – without whom there would be no light!

Below are the answers to my most frequently asked questions. If your question isn't listed, please feel free to get in touch via joannawatson.co.uk/contact and I will do my best to answer it.

*Joanna Watson*

- **I really enjoyed reading *It's All About the Light*. How can I help promote it?**

There are three main ways you can help promote this book:

a) Give a favourable word-of-mouth recommendation to your friends, relatives, colleagues, neighbours, churches and others about it. Encourage them to buy and read it. Buy copies for them as gifts!

b) Write favourable reviews for Amazon, Goodreads and whichever bookstore you used to purchase your copy. (Make it easy and put the same review on each site!) Amazon, because – even if you didn't buy the book through them – it's where many people go when they want to buy books; Goodreads, because Amazon takes Goodreads reviews into account when determining book rankings.

c) Use social media to promote *It's All About the Light* to your followers. On Instagram and Facebook, use the handle @joannawatsonwrites to tag Joanna, and the hashtag #ItsAllAbouttheLight to promote the book.

**I would love my friends / family / church to read *It's All About the Light*. How can I get hold of additional copies?**

*It's All About the Light* is available from all good bookshops, both online and in the real world. But signed copies are only available from Joanna's website shop at joannawatson.co.uk/shop. (They also include a personalised message of encouragement, as well as an author signature!)

**I would love Joanna to teach the principles contained in *It's All About the Light* to my church / other group. How can I invite her?**

Please invite Joanna to teach by emailing her through her website contact page at joannawatson.co.uk/contact.

**I would love Joanna to speak at my event / church service / conference / festival. What topics does she speak about and how can I invite her?**

The topics that Joanna speaks about are listed on her website speaking page at joannawatson.co.uk/speaking. If you want to invite her to speak on one or more of those topics, please email her through her website contact page at joannawatson.co.uk/contact.

**Does Joanna have any other teaching material that I can read? If so, where can I find it?**

Yes! Joanna writes a regular "*thought for the month*" devotional reflection that she shares with her monthly newsletter subscribers. You can subscribe to receive these via her website at joannawatson.co.uk/subscribe. You can also read her "*thought for the month*" archives on her website blog at joannawatson.co.uk/blog.

**I would love to read *Light Through the Cracks*, the book that has provided the learning on which this book is based. What is it about and how can I get hold of it?**

*Light Through the Cracks* contains ten true modern-day miracle stories, united by a common theme: all of them feature ordinary people who encounter God in extraordinary ways, in the midst of tough times.

Starting with her own dramatic story of the car accident that could have left her dead or paralysed, Joanna writes authentically and compellingly of how God breaks in when life turns tough.

Other stories include: cancer disappearing without trace; a premature baby confounding the medical predictions about his prognosis; a teenager seeing her long-term debilitating illness vanish in an instant; and a church receiving cash out of thin air, ensuring it survives the threat of closure.

The stories don't all have happy endings. They are raw, real and messy. But all of them raise faith, build hope and encourage readers to look for God in their own challenging situations.

*Light Through the Cracks* is available from all good bookshops, both online and in the real world. But if you buy your copy from Joanna's website shop at joannawatson.co.uk/shop, she will sign it with a personalised message.

**Other than in her book, *Light Through the Cracks*, does Joanna have any additional "*light through the cracks*" stories that I can read? If so, where can I find them?**

Yes! All Joanna's "*light through the cracks*" stories can be found on her website blog at joannawatson.co.uk/blog. If you subscribe to receive Joanna's monthly newsletter, you will be notified of all new "*light through the cracks*" stories as Joanna captures them on her blog. You can subscribe at joannawatson.co.uk/subscribe.

**I have my own "*light through the cracks*" story. Would Joanna be interested in it?**

Yes! If you have faced a tough time, and if God has broken into it, you have a "*light through the cracks*" story and Joanna would love to hear about it. Please get in touch by emailing her via her website contact page at joannawatson.co.uk/contact.

If it is appropriate, she may even consider sharing it on her blog.

**Is Joanna writing any more books? If so, how can I find out about them?**

Yes! Joanna has several more books in the pipeline. To be the first to hear about her new books, you need to be subscribed to receive Joanna's monthly newsletter. You can subscribe at joannawatson.co.uk/subscribe.

**How can I stay in touch with Joanna?**

The best way to stay in touch with Joanna is through her monthly newsletter, which you can subscribe to receive at joannawatson.co.uk/subscribe. Each newsletter contains a "*light through the cracks*" story, a "*thought for the month*" devotional reflection, and all Joanna's latest speaking and writing news.

**How can I connect with Joanna on social media?**

Joanna is on Instagram and Facebook, where her handle is @ joannawatsonwrites. She would love you to follow her there.

**How can I support Joanna and her ministry?**

Joanna is a recognised Christian worker with Stewardship, an organisation that matches generous Christians with ministries that need their financial support. If you would like to see Joanna continue to write, speak and raise faith in Jesus for the seemingly impossible, please consider a one-off donation, or setting up a regular gift, by going to stewardship.org.uk/partners/joannawatson.

# Acknowledgements

God has given me an incredible team of people who have helped me bring this book to birth, and all of them deserve to be thanked.

My heartfelt thanks starts with all those who entrusted me with their stories for my first book, *Light Through the Cracks*. Thank you for letting me draw out the learning from your experiences, so that others can find God in their own tough times, just as you did in yours. Thank you for your willingness to let me mention your stories in this book, and thank you for verifying the factual accuracy of each reference.

Huge thanks to those who read my first book, *Light Through the Cracks*, and got in touch, either to seek my advice for how to find God in their own tough times, or to suggest I create content to help facilitate reflection or discussion, or both. Without you planting the seed of an idea, this book might not have been. I hope it lives up to your expectations!

Thanks to Lee Abbey Devon for inviting me to speak in May 2024. Without the timing of that invitation, I would not have written the series of talks that are now adapted and incorporated into this book. Thanks also to the guests who were with me that week at Lee Abbey, for your encouraging feedback on my talks.

My sincere thanks go to J.John for providing *It's All About the Light* with such a beautiful Foreword. I knew you were the right person to ask! I am also grateful to all my wonderful endorsers for giving freely of their time, in the midst of busy schedules, to read and review this book. I so appreciate your willingness to publicly affirm what I have written. Thank you.

Thank you to Linda and Garry Currin for providing me with a beautiful place where I could hide away, with God, to write this book in peace. Thank you to Mike Beaumont for all your theological advice, particularly when I was grappling with the original Hebrew and Greek in the biblical texts. Your wisdom and insights definitely helped strengthen the manuscript. Thank you to Joy Margetts, who not only critiqued all my initial draft chapters, but also helped me frame the title and subtitle when I was toying with all sorts of ideas for what to call this book. Thank you to Natasha Woodcraft for helping me shape and hone my back cover blurb.

Huge thanks to all those who helped me consolidate the *Digging Deeper* sections of each chapter. This includes my beta readers, those who beta tested the questions and exercises, or both – especially Graham, Alex, Sarah and Joy. Reni, for coming up with some wonderful worship song ideas. Helen and Ed, for suggesting suitable books for further reading where I was stuck for ideas.

I am enormously grateful to my family and friends. You have believed in this book from the beginning, and refused to let me walk away when I wanted to give up. Special thanks to Anne, Susann, Nicole, Des and Susan, for your invaluable spiritual insights and support. Your unwavering encouragement and faith-filled prayers have been incredible, and I so appreciate how you always point me to Jesus. Thanks, too, to Adrian, for always going above and beyond; to Dilly, Mary, Marianne, Jackie and Helen for regularly checking in on me; to Liz and Claire, for your faith-filled prayers; and to Hywel, Kay, Leila and Mike for holding me accountable in such a loyal and supportive way.

I count it a privilege to be part of two writing communities – Kingdom Story Writers and the Association of Christian Writers – and I am grateful for all my writer friends in both. Thanks especially to Joy, Joy, Natasha, Rachel and Alex for freely giving me your wise counsel, and peer support, in the moments when I have wondered whether this book would ever get completed.

Thanks also to all my readers – for reading my book, *Light Through the Cracks*, the blog on my website, my monthly newsletters, my social media posts, and all the other forums where my writing can be found. The fact you enjoy reading what I write is what keeps me writing, and I am so grateful for all your online reviews, comments, likes and shares. Thank you!

I also want to thank my publishing team for enabling me to bring this book to birth: Malcolm Down for supporting the idea for this book, even before I put metaphorical pen to paper, as well as your constant calm reassurance. Sheila Jacobs for your editorial review of my initial draft book manuscript, and your suggestions for improvement, which definitely strengthened the manuscript. Louise Stenhouse for weeding out all my excess commas and other typos through your painstaking line editing. Lydia Jenkins for your proofreading. Angela Selfe for your formatting and layout of the text. And Sarah Grace for conceptualising, and Esther Kotecha for designing, the best possible front cover that encapsulates the book.

Finally, my biggest thanks go to Jesus. It's you that means *It's All About the Light.*

# About The Author

Joanna Watson is an inspirational British Christian writer, speaker and author of the best-selling book, *Light Through the Cracks: How God Breaks In When Life Turns Tough,* which contains ten true modern-day miracle stories – starting with the dramatic American car accident that could have left her dead or paralysed.

Joanna is known for her authentic communication style, her Bible-based teaching and her compelling story-telling. She is regularly invited to speak at churches, conferences and festivals; to contribute to podcasts, radio and TV programmes; and to facilitate training workshops and retreats, for churches and charities.

Her passion is to inspire and equip people to find, stretch and strengthen their faith in Jesus, for the seemingly impossible, in the midst of tough times. She regularly writes and speaks about miracles, and about the themes covered in *It's All About the Light: How to Find God in Tough Times.*

By background, Joanna trained and qualified in advocacy, initially in law and later in international development. She lives in Oxfordshire in the UK, but her work and other travels have taken her to more than 50 nations over the last 25 years.

She loves strong coffee, good books and long walks.

You can connect with Joanna at www.joannawatson.co.uk.

# Also by Joanna Watson

*Light Through the Cracks* contains ten true modern-day miracle stories, united by a common theme: all of them feature ordinary people encountering God, in extraordinary ways, in the midst of tough times.

Starting with the story of her car accident in the USA, which could have left her dead or paralysed, Joanna Watson writes authentically and compellingly of how God breaks in when life turns tough.

Each story raises faith, builds hope, and encourages readers to look for God's "*light through the cracks*" in their own challenging circumstances.

www.ingramcontent.com/pod-product-compliance
Lightning Source LLC
LaVergne TN
LVHW020044110826
845155LV00029B/628

*9781917455572*